POSTMODERN ARCHITECTURE

POSTMODERN ARCHITECTURE

LESS IS A BORE

OWEN HOPKINS

6
LESS IS A BORE

12
POSTMODERN ARCHITECTURE

218
QUOTE REFERENCES

222
INDEX

LESS IS
A BORE

"The doctrine 'less is more' bemoans complexity and justifies exclusion for expressive purposes. But architects can exclude important considerations only at the risk of separating architecture from the experience of life and the needs of society. Blatant simplification means bland architecture. Less is a bore." So wrote the great American architect and theorist Robert Venturi in **Complexity and Contradiction in Architecture** (1966), one of the most influential architectural theses of the second half of the twentieth century. Even those who reject Venturi's ideas cannot help but be affected by them, given their impact on almost every facet of contemporary architectural culture.

Venturi was writing at the height of so-called International Style Modernism, which by that time had spawned countless near-identical steel-and-glass towers in cities across the globe. Yet in his critique, Venturi went back to source, to the German-American émigré architect Mies van der Rohe, whose dictum "less is more" had come to epitomize this style. In particular, Venturi cited Mies's highly influential pavilions as built manifestations of this approach. His attack, however, was subtle. It wasn't that he thought Mies's pavilions, such as the Barcelona Pavilion (1929) or Farnsworth House in Illinois (1951), were necessarily bad architecture—rather, he recognized that their success derived from their very exceptionalism.

Yes, the Farnsworth House was a stunningly pure expression of Mies's ideas about form, structure, space, and materials. But it was dependent on a wealthy client, a beautiful, secluded site, and the fact that it was designed as a weekend retreat that, in terms of accommodation and facilities, was little more than one room. The problem, as Venturi saw it, was when this highly restricted architectural approach was bundled up as a universal style to be applied anywhere, irrespective of local cultures, histories, traditions, and environments, not to mention building types. After all, why should an office tower, city hall, university campus, hotel, or apartment block all look the same?

The irony of this was that when Modernism emerged in the first decades of the twentieth century, it was the polar opposite of a single, monolithic, apparently universal style. Instead, it was a raging competition of opposing styles and "–isms": Futurism, Constructivism, Cubism, Expressionism, Purism, Functionalism, Surrealism, and many more. In retrospect, and maybe even at the time, this was to be expected. At the root, the very idea of Modernism can be understood as the cultural response to the new conditions of modernity: industrialized production; the division of labor; Fordism; and the new social and democratic structures that ensued. Modernism was a way of making sense of this time of acute flux, meeting this complexity not with one single style, theory, or approach, but various and competing Modernisms all aiming in their own way to shape an uncertain future.

Pluralism is the natural and necessary cultural condition at such times, just as it was decades later with the emergence of Postmodernism against the backdrop of an equivalent social, economic, political, and technological shift. If Modernism was the cultural response to a world defined by industry, production, urbanization, and the nation state, Postmodernism embodied the shift towards one of post-industrialization, consumption, de-urbanization, and globalization. Postmodernism heralded the final unraveling of the postwar global order that at the same time would yield new cultural and political possibilities: Pop art, pop music, ubiquitous television, the media saturation of images, post-colonialism, the environmental movement, identity politics, and a new agency for minorities and the marginalized. Venturi advocated for an architecture that would both reflect and perhaps even help make sense of this new world: an architecture that reveled in its complexities and contradictions, rather than trying to solve them.

One of the striking things, when looking across the history of architecture, is the way certain styles hold sway, often for long periods of time—from the classical and Gothic to the Beaux-Arts and International Style. To take something like the Gothic, its preeminence during the medieval period was due, to a large degree, because it was simply how one built at that time. In this regard, it wasn't a style in any modern sense—architecture was Gothic, and vice versa. Moving further forward, as architecture became a mode of expression available not just to the church or state, or even nobility, but to the merchant and middle classes, and the companies and corporations they worked for, questions of taste and fashion, as well as politics and economics, came increasingly into play. And as architecture's stylistic and representational terms of reference increased, so there emerged a corresponding urge among some architects to codify and control, of meeting the complexity of the world with imposed order.

In this regard, the universal language of International Style Modernism was not that much of a conceptual leap from the formal and educational strictures of Beaux-Arts classicism. The difference for Modernism, however, was the belief in the transcendent validity of its values and ideals. In the context of the postwar social democracies of the Western world, this became allied with the social and political aspirations of those countries, a consensus built around a mixed economy and welfare state that was signed up to by both the political left and right. If architecture could be a tool for social transformation, then architects had the power to remake society. Modernism was, therefore, not just a style but, to use the phrase popularized by Postmodern theorists, a grand narrative—a collective endeavor to bring about a better world. Given the profound impact that Modernist architecture and planning had on towns and cities across the world, it was certainly the most visible, and arguably transformative, grand narrative of the twentieth century.

When the Modernist project inevitably failed to meet the often-utopian aspirations of its initiators and participants, it was no surprise that it was subject to attack. What was surprising was how many architects held out, clinging to Modernist orthodoxy, even as the ideological basis on which it was built unraveled beneath them: that the postwar global order and record economic growth would continue forever; that energy would be cheap and abundant in perpetuity; and that architecture could serve as an instrument for social transformation. Many architects were reluctant to let go of the grand social mission that they saw as underlying a particular Modernist aesthetic. Even today, decades later, there remains a very strong tendency among architects to close ranks stylistically, and shun anything out of the ordinary.

The persistent critique of Postmodernism from the political left holds that it saw architecture cast off its social mission to embrace commerce and (neoliberal) capitalism. Postwar collectivism and solidarity were replaced (in the UK) by Margaret Thatcher's dictum that "There's no such thing as society." But this is based on two obvious falsehoods. Firstly, while many on the political right exploited the turning of the tide against Modernism by attacking the policies with which it had been synonymous, notably council housing, Venturi's critique of Modernism was explicitly architectural, questioning on a more philosophical level his profession's ability to create buildings that reflected the complexity of (post) modern life. Secondly, and more importantly, Postmodernism argued that without aesthetic variety and stylistic disunity, without color, ornament, and historical allusion, and without the freedom to look beyond a narrow formal vocabulary, any chance of architecture having any positive social effect, let alone remaking the world, was impossible. One of Modernism's follies was the simplistic equation that the grand public policy aspirations of the postwar era—mass state housing, universal education, and healthcare—required equally grand architectural and urban solutions, and that for a building to be rational, or reflect a rational policy, it needed to appear rational and resort solely to ninety-degree angles, prioritizing truth to materials and form follows function. The great tragedy of the past forty years is that the discrediting of this architectural approach has led to the discrediting of the politics it embodied—but this is Modernism's fault, not Postmodernism's.

Venturi's critique of Modernism brought all of its overheated ideas and rhetoric back to street level, the very urban unit it had sought to eliminate, and as a result quietly turned all Modernist orthodoxy on its head. In this, Venturi's theoretical position reflected what was happening quite literally on the ground in grassroots activism. Most notable were the campaigns led by Jane Jacobs and others in New York's Greenwich Village against the "urban renewal" proposals of city planner Robert Moses, which would have radically transformed much of Lower Manhattan. Jacobs's experience fed into her seminal book **The Death and Life of Great American Cities** (1961) in which she argued for the value of dense, mixed-use urban districts that created a vital network of social and economic relations, which were destroyed through Modernist planning. There was, Jacobs observed, often a social and economic logic underlying urban and architectural disorder.

However, it wasn't just the complex realities of the street and cities as they existed that Modernists objected to, but values they embodied as architecture of the past. The issue wasn't that Modernists rejected history (aesthetically and ideologically—although many did), it was that Modernism claimed to exist outside of history, that all of the questions of architecture and city planning had finally been answered and resolved into universal principles that could be applied any time, any place.

Therefore, for Venturi to advocate for complexity and contradiction in architecture and then, as he did in his book, explore examples of this tendency across history, was doubly radical. Venturi looked to architects as diverse as Gaudí, Hawksmoor, Lewerentz, Borromini, Soane, Nash, Asplund, and Kahn for examples of, in his words, "the difficult whole": tactics that he advocated for architecture in the present. In this way, Venturi's Postmodernism did not emerge in a vacuum, simply as a critique of International Style Modernism; rather, it was an argument for something that had always existed in the history of architecture, and indeed in its greatest works, which Modernism had consciously marginalized, and in which it, itself, had been an aberration.

So while 1970s and 80s Postmodernism has to be understood in relation to the context of that particular moment, it was also the manifestation of a more fundamental sensibility that can be found in all times and all periods. Postmodernism's certain recurring aesthetic tropes—color, surface, historical reference, and so on—were really the manifestation of the sensibility's essential eclecticism, the belief of meaning over muteness, context over introspection, fragmentation over unity, doubt over certainty, and contingency over universality.

If Postmodernism is representative of any political position it is a liberal one—which is vital to distinguish from neoliberalism, where value is simply a financial indicator, and a libertarianism, in which it's every (usually) man for himself. Postmodernism is about freedom of expression, of meaning, and identity. It's about reveling in disorder, contingency, and complexity, about breaking down hierarchies, and about celebrating the marginal, overlooked, or oppressed. It sees every facet of our existence become a cultural act, and culture imbued in the very core of our individual and collective beings. Postmodernism is not an argument for relativism, but for the very value of pluralism, permissiveness, and un-thought of possibility.

Inevitably Postmodernism faced a backlash, frequently written off as a silly stylistic game or simply tasteless and ugly, in contrast to "serious" architecture—whatever that meant. By the late 1990s, Postmodernism was almost a dirty word, one that no self-respecting architect would dare mutter. Despite this, its legacy has been pervasive. Issues of place, context, and architectural meaning that have their origins in Postmodern theory have been internalized as part of nearly every architect's thinking—even if they don't necessarily realize or appreciate it.

However, at the same time, for example in London, these concepts have been subverted into the creation of a banal and reductive "New London Vernacular." In short, the equation made by planners across the city is that if a building is clad in brick then it is somehow "in keeping" with London as a city of brick, and that the project should be waved through, even if it is architecturally, and in urban terms, a disaster on every other level. "In keeping" in this context is little more than a decoy for overdevelopment, with the pernicious corollary of fostering a broader culture that disallows anything out of the ordinary. In contrast to this, architects' perennial hand-wringing over government and princely promotion of traditional design rather misses the point.

The aspect of Postmodernism that is hard to appropriate is, of course, its built legacy. As Postmodern buildings reach the age at which they can be considered historic monuments and given statutory protection from alteration and demolition, in an echo of their original radicalism, they pose important questions for how we ascribe value to architecture and privilege authorship. The history of conservation movements runs parallel to that of Modernism, and is in many ways a reflection of its value systems, with originality, authenticity, and fixedness conceived against the Postmodern attributes of the derivative, contingent, or transient. Beyond single buildings, the challenge Postmodernism poses to this ideology is even more profound with urbanism. In stark contrast to Modernist planning, when Postmodern urbanism is done well you almost don't even notice it—a tweak rather than a remaking of the functioning of the city. And of course, given the Postmodern obsession with ruins, it's almost as if many of its buildings yearn for that state. The provocation here is ultimately about architecture's relationship to time, with Postmodernism taking the position that buildings aren't meant to last forever, but are transient things, built for the here and now, and surviving, if they do, not physically but in cultural memory.

After the backlash of the 1990s and 2000s, Postmodernism and the sensibility it heralds are coming back to center stage. Architecture schools are once again becoming places of color, bold formal statements, eclecticism, ornament, decoration, meaning, and allusion to the past. This is even now beginning to filter into practice, with a growing number of usually still quite small, though intensely photogenic projects, revealing just how dreary and aesthetically moribund mainstream architecture has become.

One of the rather perplexing, though also instructive, things about the Postmodernism revival is the way it follows the recent resurgence of interest in Brutalism. At least a part of the Brutalist revival directly relates to present social and political concerns, notably the housing crisis, with those on the political left looking at an era when the state provided housing for all and recasting Brutalism as its most radical embodiment. In this context Postmodernism is Brutalism's antithesis: light, ironic, the essence of 1980s individualism and politics.

While one would be hard-pushed to detect a Brutalist revival in architecture—clients, it seems, are still put off by the perceived dystopian connotations of raw concrete—there are perhaps some similarities in why we are looking again at these two very different styles. Most notable is the fact that the generations leading the reassessments are those too young to have been indoctrinated against them. Also important is how photogenic and image-friendly each style is, albeit in different ways.

While some observers are drawn to Brutalism for its inferred social and political underpinnings, for the much larger group of revivalists it's really about aesthetics and the moody black-and-white photographs of raw concrete that are readily shared online. Shorn of its social and political agenda, one might even see this aestheticizing of Brutalism as really just an act of Postmodernism, which after all was not a rejection of Modernism but, in the word used by its foremost architectural theorist, Charles Jencks, its "transcendence."

Yet, while Postmodernism might be able to assimilate the Brutalist revival, the era of grand narratives that gave birth to the style in its original incarnation is making a comeback in contemporary politics and culture. Whether this is a narrative of a more or less unreconstructed socialism attempting to serve up long discredited ideas to a new generation, or narratives of nationalism or even race, we are seeing the grand narrative return with a vengeance. Standing in the midst of such a moment, it's always hard to make much sense of it, but the incipient revival of Postmodernism perhaps does give us a clue.

Just as Postmodernism, like Modernism before it, originally emerged at a time of political and economic transformation, of one system—neoliberalism—supplanting the mixed economy of the postwar years, its return points to the fact that we are undergoing another seismic transition. After being mortally wounded in 2008, the economic and political order that has held for forty years is entering its death throes as a new economic order slowly comes into view. Whether one calls this the fourth industrial revolution, or some kind of post-capitalist system, we already have a clear sense of its makeup: a post-work, post-digital economy built around automation, sharing, and the blurring of physical and digital realities.

The question that ensues is, what role can architecture play in this? And can it bridge the divide between being a passive reflection of this moment of flux to become an active player? To answer, we need to look back as well as forward. Although post-war Modernism did succeed in improving the material conditions of millions of people around the world, its folly was to believe that architecture alone could change the world. As the utopia that architects and planners promised failed to materialize, this belief fatally opened it up to a critique that was in its own way equally determinist: that architecture alone was at fault for the social ills of council estates or the banal steel-and-glass towers populating our city centers. Postmodernism was a way out of this bind in the 1970s and 80s and it offers us a way out today. It is only by being true to itself, by reveling in complexity and contradiction, and embracing a culture of pluralism and permissiveness, that architecture might achieve its fullest and most meaningful expression—and maybe even change the world. After all, less is a bore.

Owen Hopkins

This book brings together a group of over two hundred buildings from across the world that make striking use of color, ornament, bold forms, and diverse references, and which in differing ways reflect and embody a Post-modern sensibility. Ranging in date, building type, and location, the selection includes a number of well-known, canonical examples of Postmodernism, as well as some more surprising or unexpected inclusions. The intention is not to present an historical survey, but to reveal and celebrate architectural maximalism in all of its forms, and in doing so provoke and inspire the next generation of architects and designers.

Interspersed among the buildings are quotations from a range of cultural figures associated with Postmodernism in some way, or whose work has provided some kind of inspiration or backdrop to the movement. These quotations provide both context and counterpoint. Some are rather more condemnatory than complimentary. Yet this is wholly fitting for a movement that revels in provocation and very often defines itself against a moribund status quo. 'If They're Shooting at You, You Know You're Doing Something Right'.

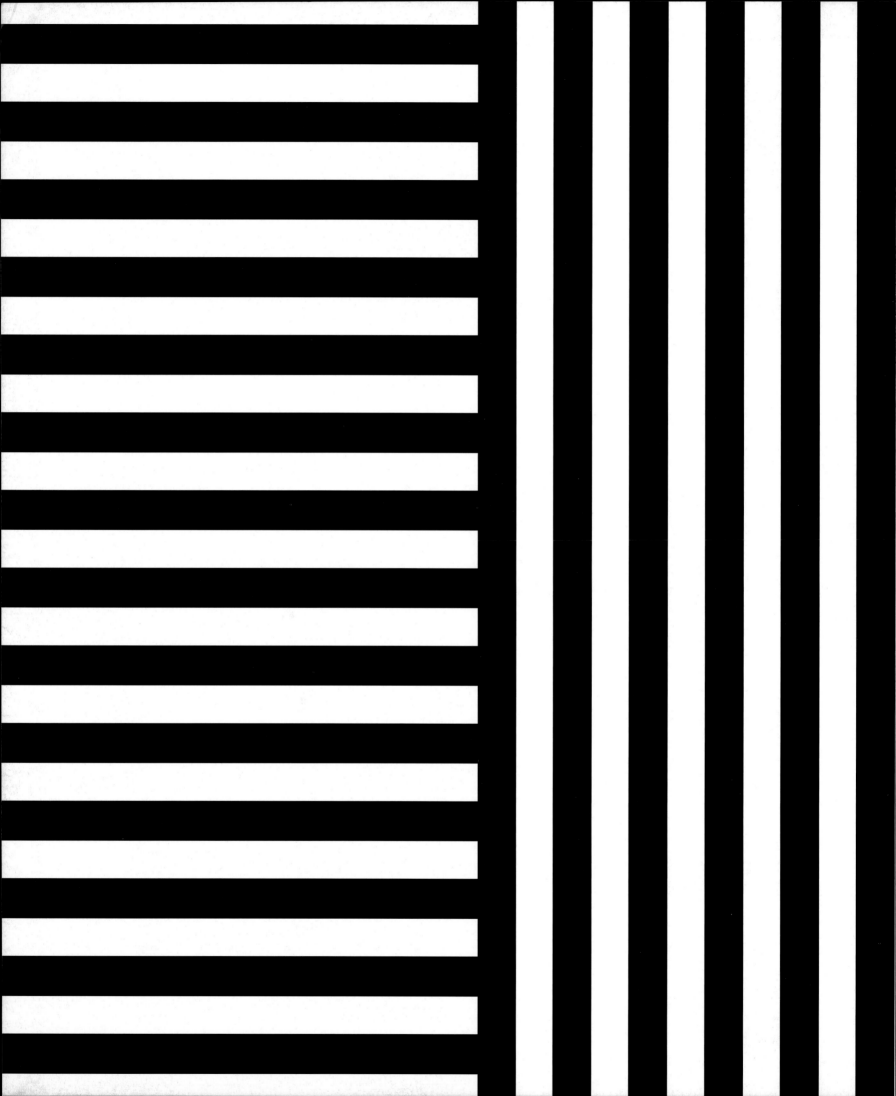

[POSTMODERNISTS ARE] AMUSING AND PERFECTLY SELF-CONSCIOUS CHARLATANS.

NOAM CHOMSKY

→ **ARATA ISOZAKI:** Team Disney Building,
Orlando, Florida, USA, 1990

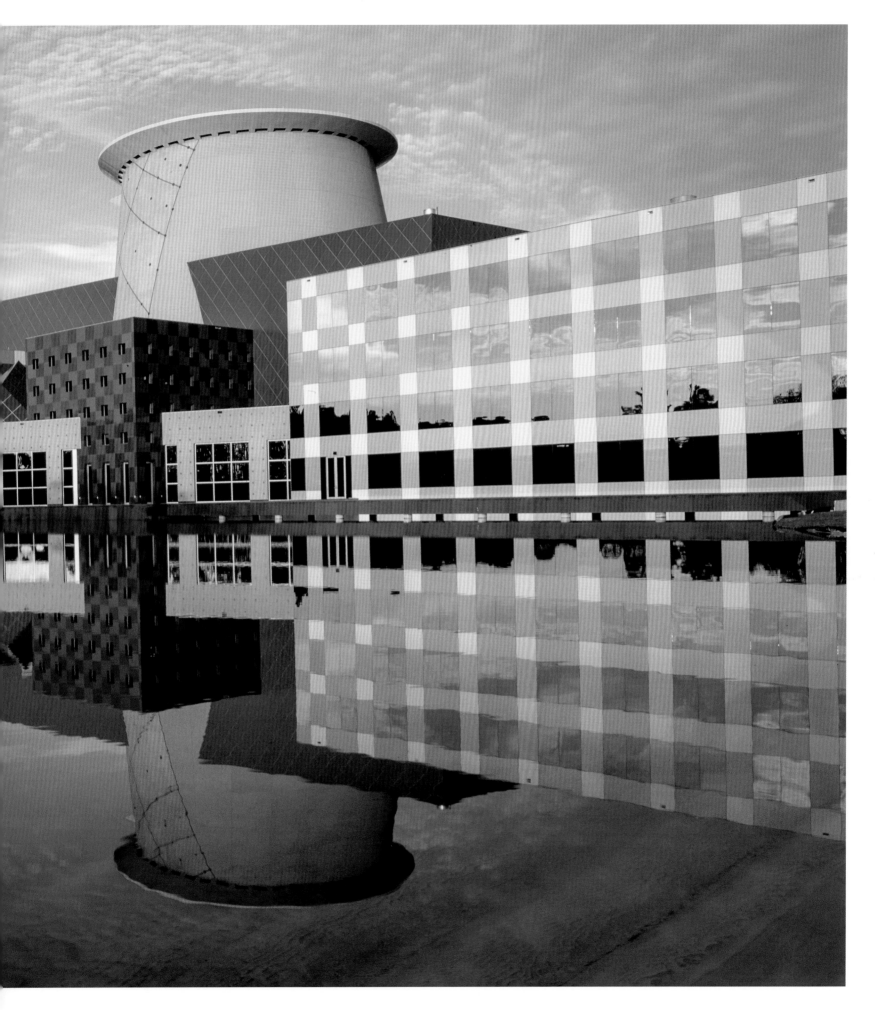

Viewed from a certain distance and under good light, even an ugly city can look like the promised land.

Léon Krier

↑ **SOETERS VAN ELDONK ARCHITECTEN:**
Piramides, Amsterdam,
The Netherlands, 2006

→ **MYS ARCHITECTS:** Opera Tower,
Tel Aviv, Israel, 1992

**The biggest misunderstanding of all
is that Postmodernism was an attack
on Modernism.**

Sam Jacob

↘ **MECANOO:** Amsterdam University
College, Amsterdam, The Netherlands,
2012

← **RICARDO LEGORRETA:** Monterrey Office
Building, Monterrey, Mexico, 1995

↑ **FRANKLIN D. ISRAEL:** Goldberg–Bean
House, Los Angeles, California,
USA, 1991

↑ **FRANCO PURINI AND LAURA THERMES:**
Casa del Farmacista, Gibellina, Sicily,
Italy, 1988

→ **ROBERT A. M. STERN:** Walt Disney World
Casting Center, Lake Buena
Vista, Florida, USA, 1989

↘ **SUMET JUMSAI:** Elephant Building,
Bangkok, Thailand, 1997

↘ **PHILIP JOHNSON AND JOHN BURGEE:**
Bank of America Center, Houston,
Texas, USA, 1983

**It takes moral and emotional blinders
to make a style. One must be
convinced one is right. Who today
can stand up and say: "I am right!"
Who, indeed, would want to?**

Philip Johnson

↖ **MICHAEL WILFORD & PARTNERS:** British
Embassy, Berlin, Germany, 2000

← **VITTORIO GREGOTTI:** Grand Théâtre
de Provence, Aix-en-Provence,
France, 2007

↑ **JAMES STIRLING MICHAEL WILFORD
& ASSOCIATES:** State University of
Music and Performing Arts, Stuttgart,
Germany, 1999

**Architects have always looked back
in order to move forward and we should,
like painters, musicians and sculptors,
be able to include "representational" as
well as "abstract" elements in our art.**

James Stirling

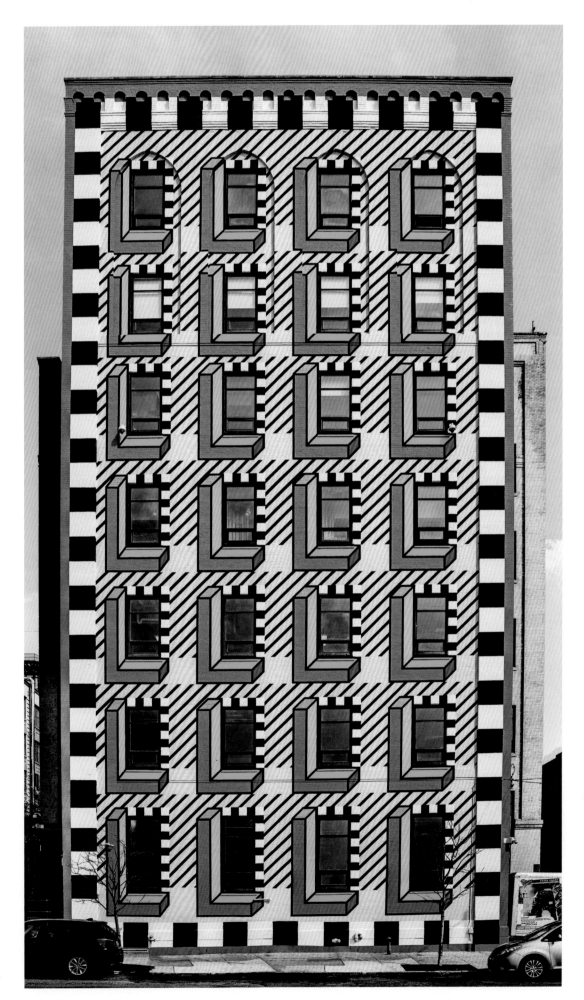

→ **STUDIO MUTT:** The Ordnance Pavilion, The Lake District, Cumbria, England, UK, 2018

→ **CAMILLE WALALA:** Industry City Mural, Brooklyn, New York, USA, 2018

↖ **ROBERT A. M. STERN:** Residence and Pool House, Llewelyn Park, New Jersey, USA, 1982

↞ **MAKOTO SEI WATANABE:** K–Museum, Tokyo, Japan, 1996

↠ **ARQUITECTONICA:** Atlantis Condominium, Miami, Florida, USA, 1982

ATROCITIES AND
ABOMINATIONS, AFFRONTS
TO HUMAN DIGNITY,
INSULTS TO ARCHITECTURAL
INNOVATION, EVIDENCE
OF SHEER LUNACY AND
TAILOR MADE TO INCITE THE
ANARCHIST TENDENCIES
IN OUR SOCIETY.

LETTER TO THE PRESS IN RESPONSE
TO AN EXHIBITION OF JAMES WINE'S
BEST BUILDINGS AT MOMA

→ **FREDDY MAMANI SILVESTRE:** Salon
de Eventos, El Alto, Bolivia, 2015

What could be a more Italian shape than Italy? And what more direct, and therefore effective, cultural reference in a piazza dedicated to the Italian community?

Charles Moore

↑ **CHARLES MOORE:** Piazza d'Italia,
New Orleans, Mississippi, USA, 1978

→ **TERRY FARRELL & PARTNERS:**
Embankment Place, London, England,
UK, 1990

The essence of Postmodernism wasn't
this style, as it emerged; it was an era,
a way of seeing and thinking. It was a
counterbalance to reason alone,
to overreliance on mechanization and
industrialization. It embraced it all, it didn't
reject it. It wasn't the beginning of a new
style, it was the mellowing of an old one.

Terry Farrell

If I have a style, I am not aware of it.
Michael Graves

↖ **MICHAEL GRAVES:** Swan Hotel, Orlando,
Florida, USA, 1989

← **VENTURI, SCOTT BROWN
AND ASSOCIATES:** Gordon Wu Hall,
Princeton, New Jersey, USA, 1983

↓ **ETTORE SOTTSASS:** Mourmans House,
Lanaken, Belgium, 2002

The Metropolis strives to reach a mythical point where the world is completely fabricated by man, so that it absolutely coincides with his desires.

Rem Koolhaas

Decoration is the origin and essence of architecture. I was told in 1955, at the beginning of my life as an architect, that my medium was both to be illiterate and devoid of metaphysical capacity. My work has been a rebellion.

John Outram

← **OMA:** Netherlands Dance Theatre, The Hague, The Netherlands, 1987

↑ **JOHN OUTRAM ASSOCIATES:** The Judge Institute, Cambridge, England, UK, 1995

Architecture can and does produce positive effects when the liberating intentions of the architect coincide with the real practice of people in the exercise of their freedom.

Michel Foucault

↑ **MARIO BOTTA:** Médiathèque,
Villeurbanne, France, 1988

→ **BERNARD TSCHUMI:** Parc de
la Villette, Paris, France, 1987

Le Corbusier was the sort of relentlessly rational intellectual that only France loves wholeheartedly, the logician who flies higher and higher in ever—decreasing concentric circles until, with one last, utterly inevitable induction, he disappears up his own fundamental aperture and emerges in the fourth dimension as a needle—thin umber bird.

Tom Wolfe

There are no hard distinctions between
what is real and what is unreal, nor
between what is true and what is false.
A thing is not necessarily either true
or false — it can be both true and false.

Harold Pinter

⇡ **KENGO KUMA:** M2 Building, Tokyo,
Japan, 1991

⇥ **SUMET JUMSAI:** Robot Building,
Bangkok, Thailand, 1986

We didn't do PoMo because we liked it.
We did it because we hated it. We were
trying to challenge our own tastes.
In telling us to "keep up the bad work,"
our hero, Robert Venturi, showed that
he understood completely.

Sean Griffiths

↑ **PAOLO ZERMANI:** Casa Zermani,
  Varano, Italy, 1997

→ **FAT:** BBC Studios, Cardiff, Wales,
  UK, 2012

I am for richness of meaning rather than clarity of meaning; for the implicit function as well as the explicit function. I prefer "both–and" to "either–or," black and white, and sometimes gray, to black or white. A valid architecture evokes many levels of meaning and combinations of focus; its space and its elements become readable and workable in several ways at once.

Robert Venturi

I see architecture not as Gropius did,
as a moral venture, as truth, but as
invention, in the same way that poetry
or music or painting is invention.

Michael Graves

↑ **ALDO ROSSI:** Celebration Place,
   Orlando, Florida, USA, 1999

⇥ **MICHAEL GRAVES:** Humana Building,
   Louisville, Kentucky, USA, 1985

I AM NOT NOW, AND NEVER
HAVE BEEN, A POSTMODERNIST
AND I UNEQUIVOCALLY
DISAVOW FATHERHOOD OF THIS
ARCHITECTURAL MOVEMENT.

ROBERT VENTURI

→ **RICARDO BOFILL:** Les Espaces
D'Abraxas, Marne La Vallée,
France, 1982

Architecture can't force people to connect, it can only plan the crossing points, remove barriers, and make the meeting places useful and attractive.

Denise Scott Brown

↑ **PAOLO PORTOGHESI, VITTORIO GIGLIOTTI, SAMI MOUSAWI AND NINO TOZZO:** Mosque and Islamic Cultural Center, Rome, Italy, 1995

→ **GRUEN ASSOCIATES AND PELLI CLARKE PELLI ARCHITECTS:** Pacific Design Center, Los Angeles, California, USA, 1975

Their so-called playful use of history
is heavy-handed, their paper-thin
pretensions misfire, no matter how solidly
enclosed or dazzlingly surfaced, these
buildings are simply not clever enough.
The problem is not that they fail to say
the same thing as the buildings they crib
from — that is neither possible in today's
world nor their avowed intention — it is
that they say nothing at all.

Ada Louise Huxtable

↑ DPZ: DPZ Offices, Miami, Florida, USA, 1988

→ ALDO ROSSI: Villa Alessi, Verbania, Italy, 1994

⇢ HELMUT JAHN: One and Two Liberty Place, Philadelphia, Pennsylvania, USA, 1987 and 1990

- **MARGARET MCCURRY:** Blue House, New Buffalo, Michigan, USA, 2003

- **WAM ARCHITECTEN:** Hotel Zaandam, Amsterdam, The Netherlands, 2010

TERRY FARRELL AND PARTNERS: TV–am
Studios, London, England, UK, 1982

MART VAN SCHIJNDEL: Oudhof,
Amsterdam, The Netherlands, 1990

JOHN OUTRAM: Isle of Dogs Storm Water Pumping Station, London, England, UK, 1988

↑ **ALDO ROSSI:** Centro Direzionale
e Commerciale Fontivegge, Perugia,
Italy, 1988

↘ **ROB KRIER:** Rauchstraße Townhouses,
Berlin, Germany, 1985

⇢ **OSWALD MATHIAS UNGERS:**
Villa Glashütte (Ungers House II),
Utscheid, Germany, 1988

It's ironic. For 30—odd years, PoMo
has been the pantomime villain stalking
the architectural scene: the scary
monster you encourage students
to stay away from.

Kester Rattenbury

MICHAEL WILFORD AND PARTNERS:
The Lowry Performing & Visual Arts
Centre, Manchester, England, UK, 2000

KISHO KUROKAWA: Wacoal Kojimachi
Building, Tokyo, Japan, 1984

HIROSHI HARA: Umeda Sky Building,
Osaka, Japan, 1993

I LIKE TO BE THE RIGHT THING
IN THE WRONG PLACE AND THE
WRONG THING IN THE RIGHT
PLACE. BEING THE RIGHT THING
IN THE WRONG PLACE AND THE
WRONG THING IN THE RIGHT
PLACE IS WORTH IT BECAUSE
SOMETHING INTERESTING
ALWAYS HAPPENS.

ANDY WARHOL

FRANK GEHRY AND CLAES OLDENBURG:
Chiat/Day Building, Los Angeles,
California, USA, 1991

← **CAN:** Lomax Studio, London, England, UK, 2018

↖ **TOMI UNGERER AND AYLA SUZAN YÖNDEL:** Kindergarten Wolfartsweier, Karlsruhe, Germany, 2002

↑ **JURGEN MAYER H, WORKAC, CLAVEL ARQUITECTOS, NICOLAS BUFFE, AND K/R:** Museum Garage, Miami, Florida, USA, 2018

Is postmodernity the pastime of an old man who scrounges in the garbage—heap of finality looking for leftovers, who brandishes unconsciousnesses, lapses, limits, confines, goulags, parataxes, nonsenses, or paradoxes, and who turns this into the glory of his novelty, into his promise of change?

Jean—François Lyotard

My particular interest is in using familiar pieces, mostly cheap pieces, putting them together in ways that they have never been before. I think that's a better way of making a revolution than just inventing a whole new crazy set of shapes.

Charles Moore

THOMAS BEEBY: Harold Washington Library, Chicago, Illinois, USA, 1991

SOM: Chase Tower, Dallas, Texas, USA, 1987

You have to give this much to the Luftwaffe: when it knocked down our buildings it did not replace them with anything more offensive than rubble. We did that.

Charles, Prince of Wales

↑ **SHIN TAKAMATSU:** Syntax Building, Kyoto, Japan, 1990

→ **RALPH ERSKINE:** The Ark, London, England, UK, 1992

My understanding of Postmodernism is/was as the grand tour for the masses, of high culture disseminated into everyday life.

Peter Saville

↑ **BEN KELLY:** The Haçienda Nightclub,
Manchester, England, UK, 1982

↝ **FRANK GEHRY:** Loyola Law School,
Los Angeles, California, USA, 1990

The stylistic phenomenon that was briefly perceived in design and architecture in the 1980s, generally called "PoMo," was a tangential blip; by no means could it be said to be the formal expression of, nor encapsulating the totality of, Postmodernism.

Terry Farrell

↑ **STANLEY TIGERMAN:** Urban Villa, Berlin,
Germany, 1988

↗ **ALESSANDRO MENDINI WITH MICHELE
DE LUCCHI, PHILIPPE STARCK AND COOP
HIMMELB(L)AU:** Groninger Museum,
Groningen, The Netherlands, 1994

In architecture as elsewhere, the active "unthinking" of Utopia is among those practices that distinguish Postmodernism from Modernism.

Reinhold Martin

**Postmodernism is Modernism
without anxiety.**

Jonathan Lethem

↑ MARIO BOTTA: Residence, Origlio,
Switzerland, 1982

→ HANS KOLLHOFF: Daimler Chrysler
Building, Berlin, Germany, 2000

↖ **CHARLES MOORE:** Beverly Hills Civic Center, Los Angeles, California, USA, 1990

← **ROBERT A. M. STERN ARCHITECTS:** Roy E. Disney Animation Building, Burbank, California, USA, 1994

↑ **ETTORE SOTTSASS:** David Kelley House, Silicon Valley, California, USA, 2000

I am very fond of ruins. They're what's left, all that is granted us by the unknown — of thoughts, of plans, of hopes.

Aldo Rossi

JOHN OUTRAM'S
INVENTION OF A SIXTH ORDER
IS AN ACT OF SHEER
ARCHITECTURAL TERRORISM.
ROBERT MAXWELL

> **Far from being Modernism's opposite, Postmodernism in architecture was the momentary rediscovery of that raging heart of modernity, the scintillating brilliance of artforms and mentalities that harness the awful beauty of what the contemporary economy can offer, in all its monstrous abundance.**
>
> Adam Nathaniel Furman

↑ **MAREK BUDZYŃSKI AND ZBIGNIEW BADOWSKI:** Warsaw University Library, Warsaw, Poland, 1998

→ **VENTURI, SCOTT BROWN AND ASSOCIATES:** Franklin Court, Philadelphia, Pennsylvania, USA, 1976

Our processes of conception must go
beyond those of architecture and design,
into the city, where the objects we may
swipe are Rome, Las Vegas, Lagos,
Tokyo, and Shanghai.
Denise Scott Brown

In the case of the BEST showrooms, each edifice was based on the assumption that people have a subliminal acceptance of certain archetypal buildings in their daily lives—suburban homes, office towers, civic centers and, especially, big box stores — so this reflex identification could be used to challenge routine expectations.

James Wines

↑ **SITE / JAMES WINES:** Best Store, Houston, Texas, USA, 1975

→ **FREDDY MAMANI SILVESTRE:** Salon de Eventos, El Alto, Bolivia, 2015

Architects in the past have tended to concentrate their attention on the building as a static object. I believe dynamics are more important: the dynamics of people, their interaction with spaces and environmental conditions.

John Portman

↑ MICHAEL GRAVES: Team Disney Building, Burbank, California, USA, 1986

⇢ MARIO BOTTA: San Francisco Museum of Modern Art, San Francisco, California, USA, 1995

They always say time changes things,
but you actually have to change
them yourself.

Andy Warhol

↑ **CZWG:** Street Porter House, London, England, UK, 1988

→ **DIMAKOPOULOS & ASSOCIATES AND LEMAY & ASSOCIATES:** 1000 de La Gauchetière, Montreal, Quebec, Canada, 1992

This [Postmodern architecture] is a transvestite architecture, Heppelwhite and Chippendale in drag.

Berthold Lubetkin

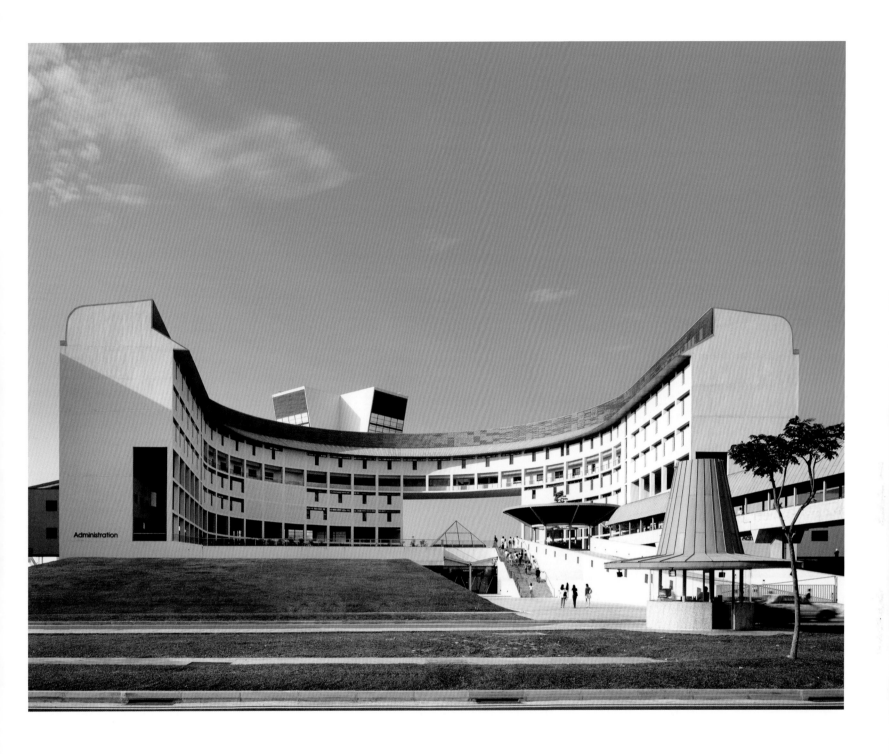

Administration

In the city, urban and monumental places,
indeed urbanity and monumentality
themselves, can occur when something
is given over by people to the public.

Charles Moore

JEREMY DIXON: Compass Point,
London, England, UK, 1988

**JAMES STIRLING, MICHAEL WILFORD
AND ASSOCIATES:** Temasek
Polytechnic, Singapore, 1988

→ **HANS KOLLHOFF:** Kop van Zuid Housing
and Commercial Building, Rotterdam,
The Netherlands, 2005

The truth, of course, is that there is no journey. We are arriving and departing all at the same time.

David Bowie

↑ **LÉON KRIER:** Village Hall, Windsor, Florida, USA, 1999

→ **LÉON KRIER:** Jorge M. Perez Architecture Center, University of Miami, Miami, Florida, USA, 2005

The city is a body and a mind—a physical
structure as well as a repository of ideas
and information.

David Byrne

I LIKE COMPLEXITY AND CONTRADICTION ... HYBRID RATHER THAN "PURE," COMPROMISING RATHER THAN "CLEAN," DISTORTED RATHER THAN "STRAIGHTFORWARD," AMBIGUOUS RATHER THAN "ARTICULATED" ... I AM FOR MESSY VITALITY OVER OBVIOUS UNITY.

ROBERT VENTURI

I think it would be stupid for us to try and tell people who are dancing in a discotheque about the problems of the world. That is the very thing they have come away to avoid.

Giorgio Moroder

→ **HELMUT JAHN:** State of Illinois Center, Chicago, Illinois, USA, 1985

Greed, for lack of a better word, is good. Greed is right, greed works. Greed clarifies, cuts through, and captures the essence of the evolutionary spirit. Greed, in all of its forms: greed for life, for money, for love, knowledge, has marked the upward surge of mankind.

Gordon Gekko

↑ **NBBJ:** Longaberger Building Headquarters, Newark, Ohio, USA, 1997

→ **RICARDO BOFILL:** 77 West Wacker Drive, Chicago, Illinois, USA, 1992

↑ **MICHAEL GRAVES:** New York Hotel, Disneyland Paris, Paris, France, 1992

→ **ARATA ISOZAKI:** Museum of Contemporary Art, Los Angeles, California, USA, 1986

⇢ **RICARDO LEGORRETA:** Fort Worth Museum of Science and History, Fort Worth, Texas, USA, 2009

[The Vanna Venturi House] ... looks like a house, in the obvious and elemental way. And yet it is far from obvious or reductive. It is rich with allusions and taught with ambiguity. It is playful and strange and familiar and deadpan, somehow all at the same time.

Charles Holland

↱ **VENTURI, SCOTT BROWN AND ASSOCIATES:**
Vanna Venturi House, Philadelphia,
Pennsylvania, USA, 1964

↳ **CHARLES JENCKS AND TERRY FARRELL:**
Thematic House, London, England,
UK, 1985

↘ **JAMES STIRLING AND MICHAEL WILFORD:**
Arthur M. Sackler Museum, Harvard
University, Cambridge, Massachusetts,
USA, 1985

Postmodernism was — is — the continuing struggle to come to terms with, and make sense of, the modern world.

Sam Jacob

FAT: Community in a Cube,
Middlesbrough, England, UK, 2012

KIKO MOZUNA: Kushiro City Museum,
Kushiro, Japan, 1983

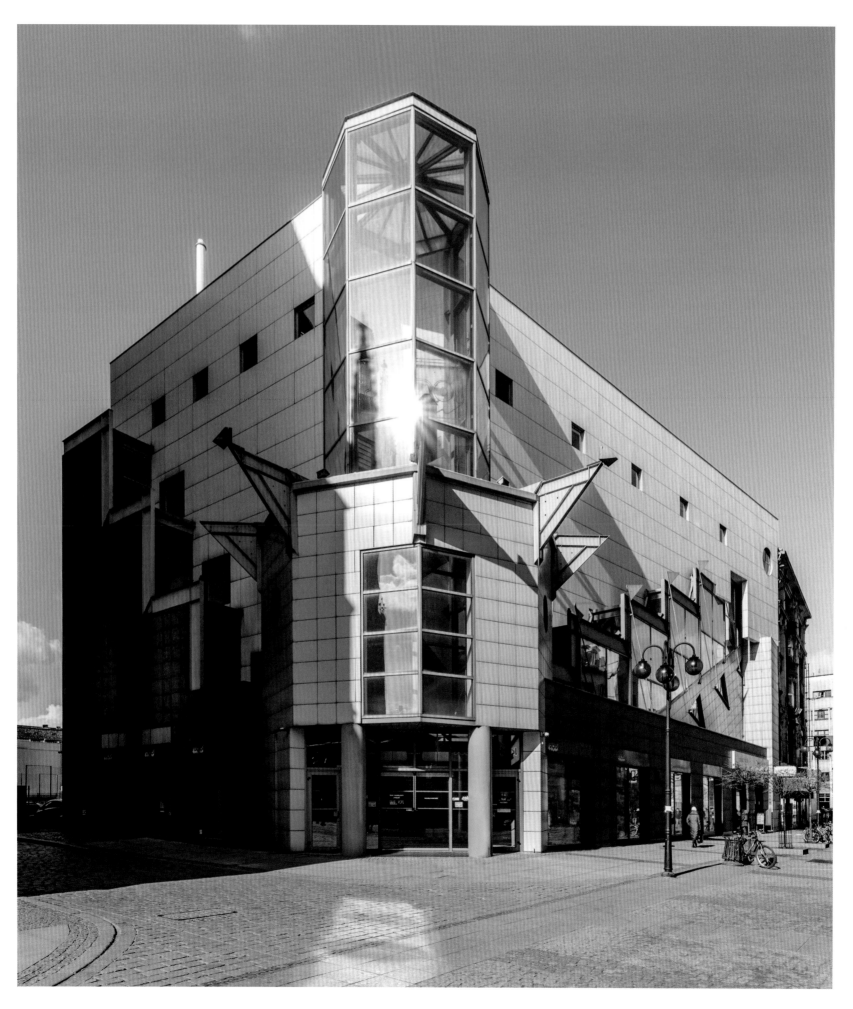

← **WOJCIECH JARZABEK:** Solpol Department Store, Wrocław, Poland, 1993

→ **KENZO TANGE:** Tokyo Metropolitan Government Building, Tokyo, Japan, 1991

↑ **MARGARET MCCURRY AND STANLEY TIGERMAN:** Boardwalk, Lakeside, Michigan, USA, 1983

→ **MICHAEL GRAVES:** St. Coletta School, Washington, D.C., USA, 2006

⤑ **CÉSAR PELLI:** Petronas Towers, Kuala Lumpur, Malaysia, 1996

SUPERFICIALITY HAS DEPTH IF UNDERSTOOD AND ACCEPTED AS THE PROFOUND DIFFICULTY OF HUMAN LIFE.

ALESSANDRO MENDINI

→ **TERRY FARRELL AND PARTNERS:**
SIS Building, London, UK, 1994

↳ **CHARLES MOORE:** Moore House,
Austin, Texas, USA, 1984

↳ **JOHN OUTRAM:** Duncan Hall, Rice
University, Houston, Texas, USA, 1996

↑ **ETTORE SOTTSASS:** The Acme House,
Maui, Hawaii, USA, 1994

⇥ **JOHN HEJDUK:** Wall House II,
Groningen, The Netherlands, 2001

⇢ **THOM MAYNE / MORPHOSIS:**
2–4–6–8 House, Los Angeles,
California, USA, 1978

↑ **SITE, JAMES WINES:** Best Products
Showroom, Miami, Florida, USA, 1979

--→ **JOHN OUTRAM ASSOCIATES:** New House,
East Sussex, England, UK, 1986

····→ **MONADNOCK:** Landmark, Nieuw–Bergen,
The Netherlands, 2015

**I'm being Postmodern, before
it's fashionable.**

Tony Wilson in **24 Hour Party People**

↑ **RICARDO BOFILL:** The Pyramid,
Le Perthus, Spanish–French Border,
France and Spain, 1976

→ **OSCAR TUSQUETS BLANCA:**
Villa Andrea, Barcelona, Spain, 1992

You know the character you need to be an architect? You need to be brave. You need to be strong. You have to have a very strong backbone. You have to have very thick skin because you're going to get beat to shit by others, without question.

Stanley Tigerman

↑ **STANLEY TIGERMAN:** The Anti—Cruelty Animal Shelter, Chicago, Illinois, USA 1981

↝ **JOHN HEJDUK:** Kreuzberg Tower, Berlin, Germany, 1988

The future could go this way, that way.
The future's futures have never looked
so rocky. Don't put money on it. Take
my advice and stick to the present. It's
the real stuff, the only stuff, it's all there
is, the present, the panting present.

Martin Amis

→ **ADNAN SAFFARINI:** Al Yaqoub Tower, Dubai, United Arab Emirates, 2013

↖ **MINORU YAMASAKI:** Helen L. DeRoy Auditorium, Detroit, Michigan, USA, 1964

← **PHILIP JOHNSON:** House on Strait Lane, Dallas, Texas, USA, 1964

↙ **GOLLINS MELVIN WARD:** Minster Court, London, England, UK, 1991

**DISNEY WORLD IS CLOSER
TO WHAT MOST PEOPLE WANT
THAN WHAT ARCHITECTS
HAVE EVER GIVEN THEM.**

ROBERT VENTURI

- **RICARDO BOFILL:** Arcades du Lac, Saint–Quentin–en–Yvelines, France, 1982

- **RALPH ERSKINE:** Lilla Bommen (Skanskaskrapan), Gothenburg, Sweden, 1989

- **WINGÅRDH ARKITEKTKONTOR:** Ting 1, Örnsköldsvik, Sweden, 2013

What has our culture lost in 1980 that the avant—garde had in 1890? Ebullience, idealism, confidence, the belief that there was plenty of territory to explore, and above all, the sense that art, in the most disinterested and noble way, could find the necessary metaphors by which a radically changing culture could be explained to its inhabitants.

Robert Hughes

← **JEREMY AND FENELLA DIXON:** St Mark's Road, London, England, UK, 1979

↑ **SHORT & ASSOCIATES:** The School of Slavonic and East European Studies, University College London, London, England, UK, 2005

↑ ARUP ASSOCIATES: Broadgate Circle, London, England, UK, 1988

↗ CZESŁAW BIELECKI AND MARIA TWARDOWSKA: TVP Headquarters, Warsaw, Poland, 2008

⤑ HANS HOLLEIN: Haas Haus, Vienna, Austria, 1990

↑ **HANS KOLLHOFF:** Main Plaza, Frankfurt, Germany, 2002

→ **CY LEE:** Chung Tai Chan Monastery, Puli, Taiwan, 2001

↙ **MOSHE SAFDIE:** National Gallery of Canada, Ottawa, Ontario, Canada, 1988

↘ **SHIN TAKAMATSU:** Pharaoh Building, Kyoto, Japan, 1984

Modern architecture died in St. Louis, Missouri, on July 15, 1972, at 3.32 p.m. (or thereabouts), when the infamous Pruitt–Igoe scheme, or rather several of its slab blocks, were given the final coup de grâce by dynamite.

Charles Jencks

**There's an element of victimhood
in Postmodernism.**

Terry Farrell

↑ **JONES AND KIRKLAND:** Mississauga Civic Centre, Missisauga, Ontario, Canada, 1987

→ **OSCAR TUSQUETS BLANCA:** Mas Abelló Housing Complex, Reus, Spain, 1988

⇢ **JOHNSON, FAIN AND PEREIRA ASSOCIATES:** Fox Plaza, Los Angeles, California, USA, 1987

OSWALD MATHIAS UNGERS AND STEFAN SCHROTH: New Pumping Station Tiergarten, Berlin, Germany, 1987

SOTTSASS ASSOCIATI: Casa Wolf, Ridgeway, Colorado, USA, 1989

ALDO ROSSI: Quartier Schützenstrasse, Berlin, Germany, 1997

Every artist joins a conversation that has been going on for generations, even millennia, before he or she joins the scene.

John Barth

THERE IS NOTHING AS TOXIC AS THE RECENTLY FASHIONABLE.

DAN GRAHAM

→ **ARQUITECTONICA:** United States
Embassy, Lima, Peru, 2012

↖ **FRANK GEHRY:** Norton House,
   Los Angeles, California, USA, 1984

↓ **RICHARD MEIER & PARTNERS
   ARCHITECTS:** Grotta House, Harding
   Township, New Jersey, USA, 1989

↘ **FRANK GEHRY:** Winton Guest House,
   Owatonna, Minnesota, USA, 1987

↘ **HANS HOLLEIN:** Retti Candle Shop,
   Vienna, Austria, 1966

↘ **HANS HOLLEIN:** Schullin I jewelery
   store, Vienna, Austria, 1974

**I'm just an advertisement
for a version of myself.**
David Byrne

ARQUITECTONICA: Pink House, Miami,
Florida, USA, 1976

VENTURI, SCOTT BROWN AND ASSOCIATES:
Provincial Capitol Building, Toulouse,
France, 1999

The alternative to the harsh responsibility
of remaining faithful to the modern
tradition lies not in pluralism, but in the
open, courageous suicide proposed
by Pop architecture, rejecting all cultural
models, all open or closed orders,
and returning to the primordial chaos,
to triviality and artifice.

Bruno Zevi

← **KAZUMASA YAMASHITA:** Face House, Kyoto, Japan, 1974

→ **MARIO CAMPI, FRANCO PESSINA AND NIKI PIAZZOLI:** Casa Maggi, Arosio, Switzerland, 1980

By its nature, the metropolis provides what otherwise could be given only by traveling: namely, the strange.

Jane Jacobs

ALESSANDRO MENDINI: Steintor Bus and Tram Stop, Hanover, Germany, 1992

MVRDV: Markthal, Rotterdam, The Netherlands, 2014

↖ **JOHN PORTMAN AND ASSOCIATES:**
Entelechy II, Sea Island, Georgia,
USA, 1986

← **ROBERT A. M. STERN:** Lang House,
Washington, Connecticut, USA, 1974

↑ **CHARLES GWATHMEY:** Gwathmey
Residence and Studio, Long Island,
New York, USA, 1965

**Postmodern architecture is
characterized by contextualism,
allusionism, and ornamentalism.**

Robert A. M. Stern

POSTMODERNISM IS THE
SUPERFICIAL AESTHETIC OF
SHODDY COMMERCIAL DESIGN,
OBSESSED WITH MONEY
AND FASHION.

RICHARD ROGERS

One can say that the city itself is the collective memory of its people, and like memory it is associated with objects and places. The city is the locus of the collective memory.

Aldo Rossi

↑ **MICHAEL GRAVES:** Denver Central Library, Denver, Colorado, USA, 1996

→ **ALDO ROSSI:** San Cataldo Cemetery, Modena, Italy, 1976

↖ **VENTURI, SCOTT BROWN AND ASSOCIATES:** Museum of Contemporary Art, San Diego, California, USA, 1996

← **ALDO ROSSI:** Residence, Seaside, Florida, USA, 1985

→ **HELMUT JAHN:** Messeturm, Frankfurt, Germany, 1991

I admire writers who can make
complicated things simple, but
my own talent has been to make
simple things complicated.

John Barth

† **TOMÁS TAVEIRA:** Amoreiras
Apartments and Shopping Center,
Lisbon, Portugal, 1985

⇥ **MICHAEL HOPKINS AND PARTNERS:**
Portcullis House, London, England,
UK, 2000

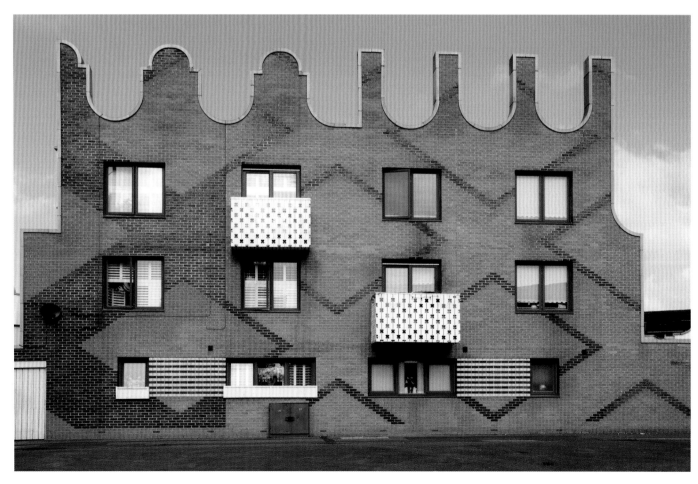

↖ **AOC:** Spa School, London, England, UK, 2011

↞ **FAT:** Islington Square, Manchester, England, UK, 2006

↠ **RALPH ERSKINE:** Byker Wall, Newcastle upon Tyne, England, UK, 1982

I'm a 'B—movie' architect.

Piers Gough

↑ **CZWG:** China Wharf, London, England, UK, 1988

⇥ **MORRIS ADJMI ARCHITECTS AND ALDO ROSSI:** Scholastic Building, New York, New York, USA, 2001

**You may have to fight a battle
more than once to win it.**
Margaret Thatcher

↑ **MARIO BOTTA:** Union Bank of
Switzerland, Basel, Switzerland, 1995

↦ **FOGGO ASSOCIATES:** 60 Queen Victoria
Street, London, England, UK, 1999

- **PHILIP JOHNSON AND JOHN BURGEE:** PPG Place, Pittsburgh, Pennsylvania, USA, 1984

- **TAKEFUMI AIDA:** Toy Block House IV, Tokyo, Japan, 1982

- **TAKEFUMI AIDA:** Toy Block House III, Tokyo, Japan, 1981

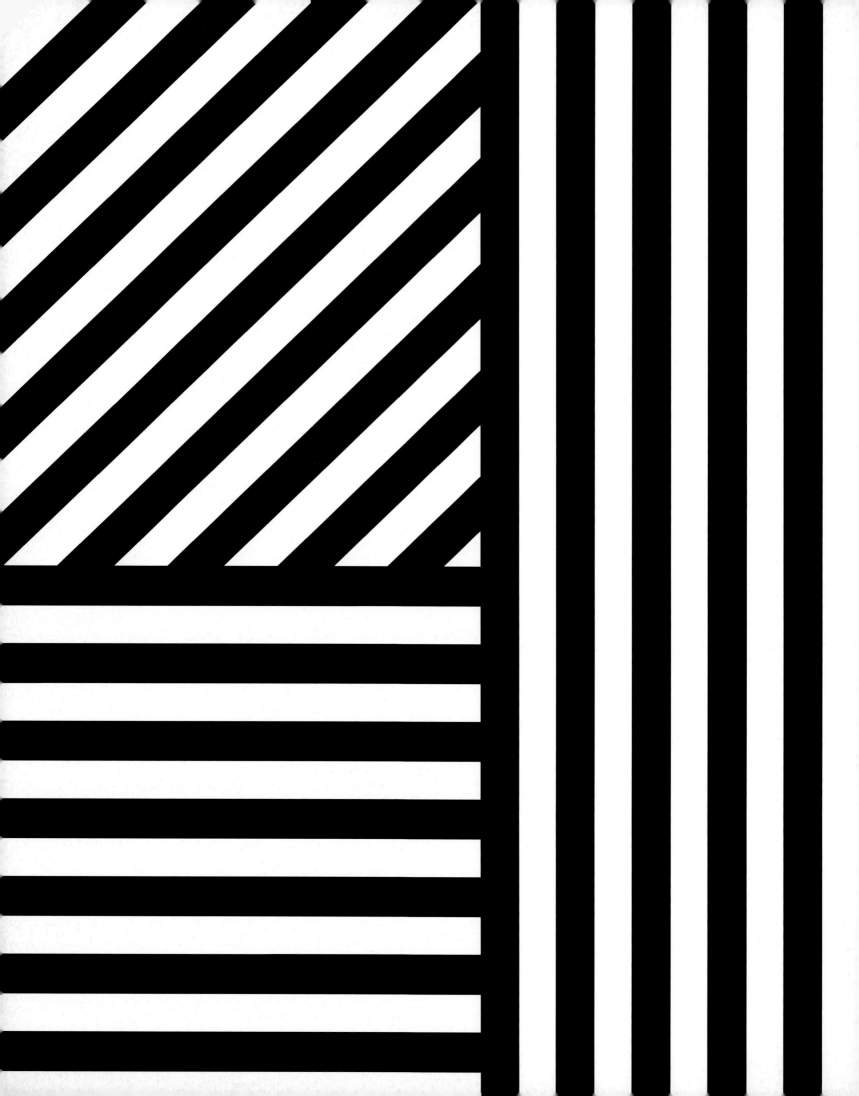

IF POSTMODERNISM MEANT
ANYTHING WAS ALLOWED,
THEN I WAS ALL FOR IT.

DAVID BYRNE

→ **RICARDO BOFILL:** Port Juvénal,
Montpellier, France, 1989

MICHAEL GRAVES: Dolphin Hotel, Orlando, Florida, USA, 1989

MICHAEL GRAVES: Condominiums, Fukuoka, Japan, 1992

GAETANO PESCE: Organic Building, Osaka, Japan, 1993

MICHAEL GRAVES: Portland Municipal Services Building, Portland, Oregon, USA, 1982

JAMES STIRLING, MICHAEL WILFORD AND ASSOCIATES: Number 1 Poultry, London, England, UK, 1997

← **PHILIP JOHNSON AND JOHN BURGEE:**
AT&T Building, New York, New York,
USA, 1984

→ **PELLI CLARKE PELLI ARCHITECTS:** World
Financial Center, New York, New York,
USA, 1988

**The desire to reach for the sky runs
very deep in our human psyche.**
César Pelli

↖ **JAMES STIRLING, MICHAEL WILFORD & ASSOCIATES, WITH WALTER NAGELI:** Braun Headquarters, Melsungen, Germany, 1992, and extension, 2001

← **GWATHMEY SIEGEL KAUFMAN ARCHITECTS:** David Geffen Foundation Building, Los Angeles, California, USA, 2000

↑ **RICARDO BOFILL:** La Place du Nombre d'Or, Montpellier, France, 1985

I feel on the fringe of Postmodern but I've always felt on the fringe. I never felt that I was Brutalist and I don't feel now that I am Postmodernist. I'm curious about Postmodernism and I'm interested, in a way, but I don't feel part of it.

James Stirling

↖ **RICARDO LEGORRETA:** San Antonio Public Library, San Antonio, Texas, USA, 1995

↤ **JOHN PORTMAN AND ASSOCIATES:** Academic Center, Georgia Gwinnett College, Lawrenceville, Georgia, USA, 2002

↦ **SHIN TAKAMATSU:** Origin III, Kyoto, Japan, 1986

← MARGARET MCCURRY: Crayola House,
Oostburg, Wisconsin, USA, 2005

↑ FAT: The Blue House, London, England,
UK, 2002

→ ETTORE SOTTSASS, ALDO CIBIC AND
BEPPE CATUREGLI: Esprit Showroom,
Düsseldorf, Germany, 1986

VENTURI, SCOTT BROWN AND ASSOCIATES: Episcopal Academy Chapel, Newton Square, Pennsylvania, USA, 2008

HANS HOLLEIN: Museum Abteiberg, Mönchengladbach, Germany, 1982

CZWG: Cascades, London, England, UK, 1988

Postmodern classicism is the new synthesis which now unites practitioners around the world as the International Style did in the twenties.

Charles Jencks

↤ **JON JERDE:** Horton Plaza, San Diego,
California, USA, 1985

↦ **DENNIS LAU & NG CHUN MAN:**
Grand Lisboa, Macau, China, 2008

QUOTE REFERENCES

Amis, Martin (b. 1949). British author and cultural and political commentator best known for his novels **Money** (1984) and **London Fields** (1989). His work centers on the excesses of late-capitalist Western society.
→ PAGE 135. From Amis's novel **Money**, published by Jonathan Cape in 1984.

Barth, John (b. 1930). American writer associated with Postmodernism and known for his complex metafictional novels such as **The Sot-Weed Factor** (1960), and what some consider to be a manifesto of Postmodernism "The Literature of Exhaustion," which was first printed in **The Atlantic** magazine in 1967.
→ PAGE 157. From Naomi Epel's book **Writers Dreaming** published by Carol Southern Books in 1993.
→ PAGE 184. From an article published in **The New York Times** in 1972 entitled "Complicated Simple Things" about Barth's writing process.

Bowie, David (1947-2016). British singer, songwriter, record producer, painter, and actor, known for his multiple incarnations, including Ziggy Stardust and the Thin White Duke.
→ PAGE 102. A well-known quotation referenced, for example, in the article "David Bowie's Most Poignant Quotes: Ageing Doesn't Faze Me—It's Death That's a Drag," published in the **Mirror** newspaper shortly after Bowie's death in 2016.

Byrne, David (b. 1952). Scottish-born American singer, songwriter, filmmaker, and writer, he was a founding member and lead singer of the band Talking Heads.
→ PAGE 103. From Byrne's essay "If the 1 Percent Stifles New York's Creative Talent, I'm Out of Here" in **Tales of Two Cities: The Best and Worst of Times in Today's New York**, edited by John Freeman and published by Penguin Books in 2015.
→ PAGE 166. A well-known quotation, referenced, for example, in **The Rough Guide to Rock**, published in 2003.
→ PAGE 155. From Byrne's "Post-Script" in the catalog of the 2011 exhibition at London's V&A Museum, **Postmodernism: Style and Subversion, 1970-1990**, edited by Glenn Adamson and Jane Pavitt.

Chomsky, Noam (b. 1928). American linguist, philosopher, cognitive psychologist, historian, and social and political activist.
→ PAGE 177. From the book **The Renaissance and the Postmodern: A Study in Comparative Critical Values** by Thomas L. Martin and Duke Pesta, published in 2016 by Routledge Press.

Farrell, Terry (b. 1938). British architect and urban designer who established one of the UK's leading international architecture practices, Farrell designed several iconic Postmodern buildings in the 1980s.
→ PAGES 35 AND 77. From Farrell and Adam Nathaniel Furman's book **Revisiting Postmodernism**, published by RIBA Publishing in 2017.
→ PAGE 151. From an interview with Farrell in **Icon** magazine (number 176), published February 2018.

Foucault, Michel (1926-1984). French philosopher and social theorist renowned for his investigations into the structures of knowledge and power.
→ PAGE 41. From "Space, Knowledge and Power," an interview with Paul Rabinow, published by Rizzoli Communications in **Skyline** in March 1982 (translated by Christian Hubert).

Furman, Adam Nathaniel (b. 1982). London-based artist and architectural designer whose work is known for its bold use of color and pattern conceived in dialogue with the past and the future.
→ PAGE 88. From Furman's 2015 essay "Style: In Defence of... Postmodernism," part of the "Style: In Defence of..." series published by Machine Books, which featured fifteen styles, including Brutalism, Expressionism, Constructivism, Parametricism, and Classicism.

Gekko, Gordon. The protagonist of **Wall Street** (1987), a film directed by Oliver Stone and starring Michael Douglas.
→ PAGE 111. In the film **Wall Street**, a young stockbroker becomes entangled in Gekko's amoral and ruthless web. The film is widely remembered for the speech delivered by Gekko in which he argues that "greed is good."

Gough, Piers (b. 1946). British architect and co-founder of CZWG, one of the leading UK architecture practices associated with Postmodernism.
→ PAGE 122. A comment made by Gough many times over the years, including in his Royal Academician profile on the Royal Academy of Arts website.

Graham, Dan (b. 1942). American artist and writer, whose work comprises a range of media and is focused on the relationship between architectural spaces and their inhabitants.
→ PAGE 153. From Graham's "Art in Relation to Architecture/Architecture in Relation to Art" essay in **Rock My Religion: Writings and Art Projects 1965-1990**, published by MIT Press in 1993.

Graves, Michael (1934-2015). American architect and educator who was one of the leading exponents of Postmodernism in the USA and best known for the Portland Building in Oregon.
→ PAGE 37. An often-cited quotation included, for example, in **Architecture: Celebrating the Past, Designing the Future**, edited by Nancy Solomon and published by Visual Reference Publications for the American Institute of Architects in 2005.
→ PAGE 46. An often-cited quotation included, for example, in **Foglio**, vol. 2, published by the Department of Architecture at Florida International University, Miami, in 2003.

Griffiths, Sean (b. 1966). British artist, academic, architect, and former director of iconoclastic practice FAT, who now practices as Modern Architect.
→ PAGE 44. From Griffiths's article "Now is Not the Time to Be Indulging in Postmodern Revivalism," published by online architecture magazine **Dezeen** on October 30, 2017.

Holland, Charles. British architect, educator, writer, and former director of iconoclastic practice FAT. Now the principal of Charles Holland Architects and professor at the University of Brighton.
→ PAGE 112. From Holland's article "Robert Venturi Opened My Eyes to Architecture," published by online architecture magazine **Dezeen** on September 21, 2018.

Hughes, Robert (1938-2012). Australian-born art critic and broadcaster, best known for the book and television series **The Shock of the New: Art and the Century of Change**.
→ PAGE 147. From Hughes's **The Shock of the New**, first published by the BBC in 1980 and republished by Thames & Hudson in 1991.

Huxtable, Ada Louise (1921-2013). Influential architecture critic for **The New York Times** and **The Wall Street Journal**, among other publications, and writer of numerous books that did much to shape public debate around architecture in the USA.
→ PAGE 53. From Huxtable's book **The Tall Building Artistically Reconsidered: The Search for a Skyscraper Style**, first published in 1984 by Pantheon.

Jacob, Sam. British architect, educator, writer, and former director of iconoclastic practice FAT, who now runs Sam Jacob Studio.
→ PAGE 15 AND 117. From Jacob's article "Postmodernism's Real Qualities Are Mean and Difficult, Yet Also Psychedelically Positive" published by online architecture magazine **Dezeen** on 13 August 2015.

Jacobs, Jane (1916-2006). American-Canadian urban theorist and activist whose book **The Death and Life of Great American Cities** was a powerful and influential critique of the principles of Modernist urban planning.
→ PAGE 173. From Jacobs's seminal book **The Death and Life of Great American Cities**, first published by Random House in 1961.

Jencks, Charles (b. 1939-2019). Critic, theorist, historian, landscape designer, author of numerous influential books on Postmodernism, and co-founder of Maggie's cancer-care centers.
→ **PAGE 150.** From Jencks's book **The Language of Post-Modern Architecture**, first published by Academy Editions in 1977.
→ **PAGE 213.** From the article "La Strada Novissima: The 1980 Venice Biennale," published in **Domus** magazine in October 1980.

Johnson, Philip (1906-2005). American architect best known for his promotion of the International Style and his role in the founding of the Department of Architecture and Design at the Museum of Modern Art in New York in 1930. He later turned to Postmodernism in the 1970s and Deconstructivism in the 1980s.
→ **PAGE 28.** From a lecture by Johnson, "What Makes Me Tick," given at Columbia University on September 24, 1975 and published by Oxford University Press in **Philip Johnson: Writings** in 1979.

Koolhaas, Rem (b. 1944). Dutch architect, urbanist, thinker, polemicist, co-founder of the international architecture practice OMA and winner of the Pritzker Prize in 2000.
→ **PAGE 31.** From Koolhaas's seminal book **Delirious New York: A Retroactive Manifesto for Manhattan**, first published by Oxford University Press in 1978.

Krier, Léon (b. 1946). Luxembourg-born architect, planner, draughtsman, and theorist. He was masterplanner of Poundbury, an experimental new town in Dorset, UK, designed according to the architectural principles expounded by HRH the Prince of Wales.
→ **PAGE 16.** From Krier's book **The Architecture of Community**, published by Island Press in 2009.

Lethem, Jonathan (b. 1964). American novelist and essayist, author of **Gun, with Occasional Music** (1994) and **Motherless Brooklyn** (1999).
→ **PAGE 80.** Often-cited quotation included, for example, in Darran Anderson's article "Revisiting Postmodernism," published in **Disegno** magazine on May 23, 2018.

Lubetkin, Berthold (1901-1990). Russian-born architect who immigrated to Britain in 1931, where he became a pioneering figure in the development of Modernism before and after World War II.
→ **PAGE 54.** Quoted from Lubetkin's Royal Gold Medal address at the Royal Institute of British Architects in 1982.

Lyotard, Jean-François (1924-1998). French philosopher and one of the leading theorists of Postmodernism, articulated in **The Postmodern Condition** (1979) among other books.
→ **PAGE 71.** From Lyotard's **The Differend: Phrases in Dispute** (originally published in French as **Le Différend** in 1983), translated by Georges Van Den Abbeele, and published by the University of Minnesota Press in 1988.

Martin, Reinhold (b. 1964). American architectural historian and professor of architecture at the Columbia Graduate School of Architecture, Planning and Preservation, where he directs the Temple Hoyne Buell Center for the Study of American Architecture.
→ **PAGE 79.** From Martin's book **Utopia's Ghost: Architecture and Postmodernism, Again**, published by the University of Minnesota Press in 2010.

Maxwell, Robert (b. 1922). Architect, writer, and educator, who taught at the Architectural Association and the Bartlett School of Architecture in the UK, and at Princeton in the USA where he was dean of architecture during the 1980s.
→ **PAGE 85.** From an article by Maxwell in the journal **Architecture Today** (November 1995) and referenced by British architect John Outram on his website, johnoutram.com.

Mendini, Alessandro (1931-2019). Italian architect and designer known for his colorful, highly patterned designs, especially furniture, that mix a range of references.
→ **PAGE 123.** From the **Design Interviews** video series (2011), which presents interviews with master designers including Richard Sapper, Ettore Sottsass, and Achille Castiglioni. The series was launched by the Museum of Modern Art, New York.

Moore, Charles (1925-1993). American architect and educator known for his stylistically bold and sophisticated approach to Postmodern architecture.
→ **PAGES 39, 72, AND 99.** From Alexandra Lange's article "Why Charles Moore (Still) Matters" published in **Metropolis** magazine, May 20, 2014.

Moroder, Giorgio (b. 1940). Influential Italian music producer, songwriter, and singer, sometimes described as the "father of disco".
→ **PAGE 106.** Well-known quotation referenced, for example, in Emerson Rosenthal's article "Original Creators: Disco's Smoothest Operator Giorgio Moroder" in **Vice** on April 23, 2012.

Outram, John (b. 1934). Maverick British architect often described as a Postmodernist but who pursues his own ideas around ornament, symbolism, and the narrative potential of architecture.
→ **PAGE 35.** Quote by Outram that appeared in publicity surrounding the historical preservation listing of his Isle of Dogs Storm Water Pumping Station in 2017. For example, Richard Waite's article "John Outram's Po-Mo Pumping Station Given Grade II* Listing" in the **Architect's Journal** on June 21, 2017.

Pelli, César (b. 1926). Argentine-American architect, whose firm, established in 1977, is responsible for some of the world's largest and most recognizable towers and commercial buildings.
→ **PAGE 203.** Often-cited quotation included, for example, in Peter Karl Kresl and Daniele Ietri's book **Creating Cities/Building Cities: Architecture and Urban Competitiveness**, published by Edward Elgar Publishing in 2017.

Pinter, Harold (1930-2008). Influential British playwright, screenwriter, director, and writer of iconic plays such as **The Birthday Party** (1957) and screenplays like **The Go-Between** (1971). Pinter was awarded the Nobel Prize for Literature in 2005.
→ **PAGE 42.** Quotation originally written by Pinter in 1958 and cited in his Nobel Lecture in 2005 on the occasion of his acceptance of the Nobel Prize for Literature.

Portman Jr. John C. (1924-2017). American architect and property developer known for his futuristic hotel designs, which characteristically feature dramatic multistory atria.
→ **PAGE 52.** From **The Architect As Developer** by John Portman and Jonathan Barnett, published by McGraw-Hill in 1976.

Rattenbury, Kester. London-based architectural journalist, critic, author, teacher, and professor of architecture at the University of Westminster, London.
→ **PAGE 63.** From Rattenbury's essay "Too Good to the True: The Survival of English Everyday Pomo" in **Radical Post-Modernism**, a special issue of the journal **Architectural Design**, 2011.

Rogers, Richard (b. 1933). British architect and one of the leading figures of High Tech architecture, along with Norman Foster and Nicholas Grimshaw.
→ **PAGE 177.** Quoted in Historic England's **Post-Modern Architecture: Introductions to Heritage Assets** published in December 2017.

Saville, Peter (b. 1955). British designer and co-founder of Factory Records for which he designed album covers for bands including Joy Division and New Order.
→ **PAGE 76.** Comment made at an event as part of a series entitled "By Design" at Sir John Soane's Museum in London on October 25, 2018.

Scott Brown, Denise (b. 1931). American architect, theorist, and urban planner who, with her late husband and partner, Robert Venturi, has been responsible for transforming contemporary thinking about architecture and cities.
→ **PAGE 52.** From an interview with Scott Brown and Venturi by Andrea Tamas, published by online architecture platform **Arch Daily** on April 25, 2011.
→ **PAGE 83.** From Scott Brown's essay "Our Postmodernism" in the catalogue of the 2011 exhibition at London's V&A Museum, **Postmodernism: Style and Subversion, 1970-1990**.

Sottsass, Ettore (1917–2007). Influential Italian designer, sometime architect, and founder of the Memphis group of designers. His furniture and interiors are among the most celebrated and recognizable examples of Postmodern design.
→ PAGE 13. From a conversation between Sottsass and Giampiero Bosoni in the catalog of the exhibition **Il Modo Italiano: Italian Design and Avant-Garde in the 20th Century** at the Montreal Museum of Fine Arts in 2006.

Stern, Robert A. M. (b. 1939). Architect and former dean at the Yale School of Architecture (1998–2016), who came to be associated with Postmodernism early in his career. In more recent years, his firm has been notable for its willingness to design in a range of styles.
→ PAGE 179. As quoted in the essay "Civitas Interruptus" by Thomas Weaver in the catalog of the 2011 exhibition at London's V&A Museum, **Postmodernism: Style and Subversion**, 1970–1990, edited by Glenn Adamson and Jane Pavitt.

Stirling, James (1926–1992). One of the most significant British architects of the latter part of the twentieth century. He was associated with Brutalism early in his career, then with Postmodernism from the late 1970s.
→ PAGE 25. From **Neue Staatsgalerie Stuttgart** published on the occasion of the opening of the building of the same name in 1984.
→ PAGE 205. From Geoffrey H. Baker's **The Architecture of James Stirling and His Partners James Gowan and Michael Wilford**, published by Ashgate in 2011.

Thatcher, Margaret (1925–2013). Transformative British politician who led the Conservative Party (1975–90) and served as Prime Minster (1979–90)—the first woman to hold the office.
→ PAGE 139. From the article "Margaret Thatcher—Business Advocate" by Nelson Davis about Thatcher's economic and business policies, published by online news site **Huffington Post** in 2013.

Tigerman, Stanley (b. 1930–2019). Chicago-based American architect and theorist known for his formally and stylistically eclectic designs.
→ PAGE 134. From Iker Gil and Ann Lui's interview with Tigerman "In Chicago, I'd Much Rather Have Better Work Than Better Friends," published by online architecture platform **Arch Daily** on 17 January 2016.

Venturi, Robert (1925–2018). American architect and theorist who, with his wife and partner, Denise Scott Brown, pioneered and popularized a Postmodern approach to architecture and cities.
→ PAGE 141. From Venturi's **New York Times** article "Mickey Mouse Teaches the Architects," published on 22 October 1972.
→ PAGE 43. From Venturi's article "A Bas Postmodernism, of Course" published in the journal **Architecture** in May 2001.
→ PAGE 45 AND 105. From Venturi's seminal **Complexity and Contradiction in Architecture**, first published in 1966 by the Museum of Modern Art, New York.

Warhol, Andy (1928–1987). American artist, film director, music producer, and leading figure of the Pop art movement.
→ PAGE 67 AND 93. From **The Philosophy of Andy Warhol (From A to B & Back Again)**, first published in 1975 by Harcourt Brace Jovanovich.

The West Wing (1999–2006). An American political television drama that was set in the West Wing of the White House during the fictional administration of President Josiah Bartlet.
→ PAGE 11. The quote is from an episode of The West Wing called "The Midterms" which was written by Aaron Sorkin and aired on October 18, 2000. It comes from a conversation between an IT repair man, Andrew Macintosh, and the President's assistant, Charlie Young; Andrew tells Charlie that the quote was something his father used to say

Wilson, Tony (1950–2007). British record label owner, radio and television presenter, and nightclub manager. One of the co-founders of Factory Records and the founder and manager of the former Haçienda nightclub in Manchester, UK.
→ PAGE 155. From the film **24 Hour Party People** (2002), a comedy-drama about Manchester's music scene in the 1980s. The film focuses on the bands and characters associated with Factory Records, such as Joy Division, New Order, and Happy Mondays, under impresario Wilson (played by Steve Coogan).

Wines, James (b. 1932). American architect, artist, and founder of SITE, an architecture and environmental design practice based in New York City.
→ PAGE 31 AND 58. Taken from a letter to the press sent by a member of the public in response to an exhibition of buildings for Best Products at the Museum of Modern Art in New York, and quoted by Wines in his essay "Arch-Art: Architecture as Subject Matter." This was published in the catalog of the 2011 exhibition at London's V&A Museum, **Postmodernism: Style and Subversion**, 1970–1990, edited by Glenn Adamson and Jane Pavitt.

Wolfe, Tom (1931–2018). American author and journalist associated with the New Journalism of the 1960s, and author of books including **The Electric Kool-Aid Acid Test** (1968) and **The Right Stuff** (1979).
→ PAGE 41. From the book **From Bauhaus to Our House** published by Farrar, Straus and Giroux in 1981. Wolfe directs his literary eye at modern architecture, which he attacks in typically elegant form for its plainness, its claims at universalism, and the philosophical pretensions of its leading lights.

Zevi, Bruno (1918–2000). Italian Marxist architect, critic, and curator. An influential figure in his home country and beyond, he was a staunch critic of classicism in contemporary architecture.
→ PAGE 167. From Zevi's essay "Pluralismo e Pop-Architettura" in the journal **L'Architettura** 143, published in September 1967.

INDEX

Page numbers in **bold** refer to illustrations

₂—₄—₆—₈ House, Los Angeles **129**
₆₈ Queen Victoria Street, London **191**
₇₇ West Wacker Drive, Chicago **109**
₁₀₀₀ de La Gauchetière, Montreal **95**

A
Academic Center, Georgia Gwinnett College, Lawrenceville **208**
The Acme House, Maui **128**
Aida, Takefumi
    Toy Block House III **193**
    Toy Block House IV **193**
Al Yaqoub Tower, Dubai **136—7**
Amis, Martin 115
Amoreiras Apartments and Shopping Center, Lisbon **184**
Amsterdam University College **18**
The Anti—Cruelty Animal Shelter, Chicago **134**
AOC, Spa School **186**
Arcades du Lac, Saint-Quentin-en-Yvelines **142—3**
The Ark, London **75**
Arquitectonica
    Atlantis Condominium **29**
    Pink House **166**
    United States Embassy **160—1**
Arthur M. Sackler Museum, Harvard University **115**
Arup Associates, Broadgate Circle **148**
AT&T Building, New York **202**
Atlantis Condominium, Miami **29**

B
Badowski, Zbigniew, Warsaw University Library **88**
Bank of America Center, Houston **23**
Barth, John 157, 214
BBC Studios, Cardiff **45**
Beeby, Thomas, Harold Washington Library **72**
Best Products Showroom, Miami **130**
Best Store, Houston **90**
Beverly Hills Civic Center, Los Angeles **82**
Bielecki, Czesław, TVP Headquarters **148**
The Blue House, London **211**
Blue House, New Buffalo **56**
Boardwalk, Lakeside **120**
Bofill, Ricardo
    ₇₇ West Wacker Drive **109**
    Arcades du Lac **142—3**
    Les Espaces D'Abraxas **50—1**
    La Place du Nombre d'Or **205**
    Port Juvénal **196—7**
    The Pyramid **132**
Botta, Mario
    Médiathèque **40**
    Residence **80**
    San Francisco Museum of Modern Art **93**
    Union Bank of Switzerland **190**
Bowie, David 112
Braun Headquarters, Melsungen **204**
British Embassy, Berlin **24**
Broadgate Circle, London **148**
Budzyński, Marek, Warsaw University Library **88**
Burgee, John
    AT&T Building **202**
    PPG Place **192**
Byker Wall, Newcastle upon Tyne **187**
Byrne, David 112, 166, 155

C
Campi, Mario
    Casa Maggi **169**
    Church of Our Lady of Fatima **96—7**
CAN, Lomax Studio **70**
Casa del Farmacista, Gibellina **20**

Casa Maggi, Arosio **169**
Casa Wolf, Ridgeway **156**
Casa Zermani, Varano **44**
Cascades, London **213**
Caturegli, Beppe, Esprit Showroom **211**
CDT Building, Bryanston School, Blandford Forum **206—7**
Celebration Place, Orlando **46**
Centro Direzionale e Commerciale Fontivegge, Perugia **62**
Charles, Prince of Wales 74
Chase Tower, Dallas **73**
Chiat/Day Building, Los Angeles **68—9**
China Wharf, London **188**
Chomsky, Noam 13
Chung Tai Chan Monastery, Puli **151**
Church of Our Lady of Fatima, Giova **96—7**
Cibic, Aldo, Esprit Showroom **211**
Community in a Cube, Middlesbrough **116**
Compass Point, London **98**
Condominiums, Fukuoka **198**
Coop Himmelb(l)au, Groninger Museum **79**
Crayola House, Oostburg **210**
CZWG
    Cascades **213**
    CDT Building, Bryanston School **206—7**
    China Wharf **188**
    Street Porter House **94**

D
Daimler Chrysler Building, Berlin **81**
David Geffen Foundation Building, Los Angeles **204**
David Kelley House, Silicon Valley **83**
de Lucchi, Michele, Groninger Museum **79**
Denver Central Library **180**
Dimakopoulos & Associates, ₁₀₀₀ de La Gauchetière **95**
Dixon, Jeremy, Compass Point **98**
Dixon, Jeremy and Fenella, St Mark's Road **146**
Dolphin Hotel, Orlando **198**
DPZ, DPZ Offices, Miami **54**
Duncan Hall, Rice University **127**

E
Elephant Building, Bangkok **22**
Embankment Place, London **35**
Entelechy II, Sea Island **174**
Episcopal Academy Chapel, Pennsylvania **212**
Erskine, Ralph
    The Ark **75**
    Byker Wall **187**
    Lilla Bommen (Skanskaskrapan) **142—3**
Les Espaces D'Abraxas, Marne La Vallée **50—1**
Esprit Showroom, Düsseldorf **211**

F
Face House, Kyoto **168**
Farrell, Terry 35, 77, 151
    Thematic House **114**
FAT
    BBC Studios **45**
    The Blue House **211**
    Community in a Cube **116**
    A House for Essex **86—7**
    Islington Square **186**
Foggo Associates, ₆₈ Queen Victoria Street **191**
Fort Worth Museum of Science and History **111**
Foucault, Michel 41
Fox Plaza, Los Angeles **155**
Franklin Court, Philadelphia **89**
Furman, Adam Nathaniel 11

G
Gehry, Frank
    Chiat/Day Building **68—9**
    Loyola Law School **77**
    Norton House **162**
    Winton Guest House **163**
Gekko, Gordon 111
Gigliotti, Vittorio, Mosque and Islamic Cultural Center **52**
Goldberg-Bean House, Los Angeles **19**
Gollins Melvin Ward, Minster Court **139**
Gordon Wu Hall, Princeton **36**

Gough, Piers 111
Graham, Dan 133
Grand Lisboa, China 215
Grand Théâtre de Provence, Aix-en-Provence 24
Graves, Michael 37, 46
   Condominiums 198
   Denver Central Library 180
   Dolphin Hotel 198
   Humana Building 47
   New York Hotel 110
   Portland Municipal Services Building 200
   St. Coletta School 120
   Swan Hotel 36
   Team Disney Building 92
Gregotti, Vittorio, Grand Théâtre de Provence 24
Griffiths, Sean 44
Groninger Museum 79
Gropius, Walter 41
Grotta House, Harding Township 163
Gruen Associates, Pacific Design Center 53
Gwathmey, Charles, Gwathmey Residence and Studio 175
Gwathmey Siegel Kaufman Architects
   David Geffen Foundation Building 204
   Rales Residence and Glenstone Museum 170—1

H
Haas Haus, Vienna 149
The Haçienda Nightclub, Manchester 76
Hara, Hiroshi, Umeda Sky Building 65
Harold Washington Library, Chicago 72
Hejduk, John
   Kreuzberg Tower 135
   Wall House II 128
Helen L. DeRoy Auditorium, Detroit 138
Holland, Charles 112
Hollein, Hans
   Haas Haus 149
   Museum Abteiberg 212
   Retti Candle Store 164
   Schullin I jewelery store 165
Horton Plaza, San Diego 214
Hotel Zaandam, Amsterdam 57
A House for Essex, Manningtree 86—7
House on Strait Lane, Dallas 138
Hughes, Robert 147
Humana Building, Louisville 47
Huxtable, Ada Louise 53

I
Industry City Mural, Brooklyn 27
Isle of Dogs Storm Water Pumping Station, London 60—1
Islington Square, Manchester 186
Isozaki, Arata
   Museum of Contemporary Art 110
   Team Disney Building 14—15
Israel, Franklin D., Goldberg-Bean House 19

J
Jacob, Sam 13, 117
Jacobs, Jane 9, 123
Jahn, Helmut
   Messeturm 183
   One and Two Liberty Place 55
   State of Illinois Center 106—7
James Stirling, Michael Wilford & Associates
   Braun Headquarters 204
   Neue Staatsgalerie 178—9
   Number 1 Poultry 201
   State University of Music and Performing Arts 25
   Temasek Polytechnic 99
Jarzabek, Wojciech, Solpol Department Store 118
Jencks, Charles 10, 151, 213
   Thematic House 112—13
Jerde, Jon, Horton Plaza 214
John Outram Associates
   New House 130
   The Judge Institute 39
John Portman and Associates
   Academic Center, Georgia Gwinnett College 208
   Entelechy II 174

Johnson, Fain and Pereira Associates, Fox Plaza 155
Johnson, Philip 21
   AT&T Building 202
   Bank of America Center 23
   House on Strait Lane 138
   PPG Place 192
Jones and Kirkland, Mississauga Civic Centre 154
The Judge Institute, Cambridge 39
Jumsai, Sumet
   Elephant Building 22
   Robot Building 43

K
K-Museum, Tokyo 28
Kelly, Ben, The Haçienda Nightclub 76
Kindergarten Wolfartsweier, Karisruhe 70
Kollhoff, Hans
   Daimler Chrysler Building 81
   Kop van Zuid Housing and Commercial Building 100—1
   Main Plaza 150
Koolhaas, Rem 31
Kop van Zuid Housing and Commercial Building, Rotterdam
   100—1
Kreuzberg Tower, Germany 135
Krier, Léon 16
   Jorge M. Perez Architecture Center 103
   Village Hall 102
Krier, Rob, Rauchstraße Townhouses 62
Kuma, Kengo, M2 Building 42
Kurokawa, Kisho, Wacoal Kojimachi Building 64
Kushiro City Museum 117

L
Landmark, Nieuw-Bergen 131
Lang House, Washington 174
Lau, Dennis, Grand Lisboa 215
Le Corbusier 41
Lee, Cy, Chung Tai Chan Monastery 151
Legorreta, Ricardo
   Fort Worth Museum of Science and History 111
   Monterrey Office Building 18
   San Antonio Public Library 208
Lemay & Associates, 1000 de La Gauchetière 95
Lethem, Jonathan 11
Lilla Bommen (Skanskaskrapan), Gothenburg 142—3
Lomax Studio, London 70
Longaberger Building Headquarters, Newark 108
The Lowry Performing & Visual Arts Centre, Manchester
   64
Loyola Law School, Los Angeles 77
Lubetkin, Berthold 34
Lyotard, Jean-François 71

M
M2 Building, Tokyo 42
McCurry, Margaret
   Blue House 56
   Boardwalk 120
   Crayola House 210
Main Plaza, Frankfurt 150
Markthal, Rotterdam 173
Martin, Reinhold 71
Mas Abelló Housing Complex, Reus 154
Maxwell, Robert 15
Mayer H, Jurgen, Museum Garage 71
Mecanoo, Amsterdam University College 18
Médiathèque, Villeurbanne 40
Mendini, Alessandro 123
   Groninger Museum 79
   Steintor Bus and Tram Stop 172
Messeturm, Frankfurt 183
Michael Hopkins and Partners, Portcullis House 185
Michael Wilford & Partners
   British Embassy, Berlin 24
   The Lowry Performing & Visual Arts Centre 64
Mies van der Rohe, Ludwig 7
Minster Court, London 139
Mississauga Civic Centre 154
Monadnock, Landmark 131
Monterrey Office Building 18

Moore, Charles 34, 52, 53
  Beverly Hills Civic Center 82
  Moore House 126
  Piazza d'Italia 34
Moore House, Texas 126
Moroder, Giorgio 116
Morphosis, 2—4—6—8 House 129
Morris ADJMI Architects, Scholastic Building 189
Moses, Robert 9
Mosque and Islamic Cultural Center, Rome 52
Mourmans House, Lanaken 37
Mousawi, Sami, Mosque and Islamic Cultural Center 52
Mozuna, Kiko, Kushiro City Museum 117
Museum Abteiberg, Mönchengladbach 212
Museum of Contemporary Art, Los Angeles 110
Museum of Contemporary Art, San Diego 182
Museum Garage, Miami 71
MVRDV, Markthal 173
MYS Architects, Opera Tower 17

N
Nageli, Walter, Braun Headquarters 204
National Gallery of Canada, Ottawa 152
NBBJ, Longaberger Building Headquarters 108
Netherlands Dance Theatre, The Hague 38
Neue Staatsgalerie, Stuttgart 178—9
New House, East Sussex 130
New Pumping Station Tiergarten, Berlin 156
New York Hotel, Disneyland Paris 110
Ng Chun Man, Grand Lisboa 215
Norton House, Los Angeles 162
Number 1 Poultry, London 201

O
Oldenburg, Claes, Chiat/Day Building 68—9
OMA, Netherlands Dance Theatre 38
One and Two Liberty Place, Philadelphia 55
Opera Tower, Tel Aviv 17
The Ordnance Pavilion, The Lake District 26
Organic Building, Osaka 199
Origin III, Kyoto 209
Oudhof, Amsterdam 59
Outram, John 33, 85
  Duncan Hall 127
  Isle of Dogs Storm Water Pumping Station 60—1

P
Pacific Design Center, Los Angeles 53
Parc de la Villette, Paris 41
Pelli, César 203
  Petronas Towers 121
Pelli Clarke Pelli Architects
  Pacific Design Center 53
  World Financial Center 203
Perez Architecture Center, University of Miami 103
Perry, Grayson, A House for Essex 86—7
Pesce, Gaetano, Organic Building 199
Pessina, Franco
  Casa Maggi 169
  Church of Our Lady of Fatima 96—7
Petronas Towers, Kuala Lumpur 121
Pharaoh Building, Kyoto 153
Piazza d'Italia, New Orleans 34
Piazzoli, Niki, Casa Maggi 169
Pink House, Miami 166
Pinter, Harold 42
Piramides, Amsterdam 16
La Place du Nombre d'Or, Montpellier 205
Port Juvénal, Montpellier 196—7
Portcullis House, London 185
Portland Municipal Services Building 200
Portman, John 52
Portoghesi, Paolo, Mosque and Islamic Cultural Center 52
PPG Place, Pittsburgh 192
Provincial Capitol Building, Toulouse 167
Purini, Franco, Casa del Farmacista 20
The Pyramid, Le Perthus 132

Q
Quartier Schützenstrasse, Berlin 157

R
Rales Residence and Glenstone Museum, Potomac 170—1
Rattenbury, Kester 63
Rauchstraße Townhouses, Berlin 62
Residence, Origlio 80
Residence, Seaside 182
Residence and Pool House, New Jersey 28
Retti Candle Store, Vienna 164
Richard Meier & Partners Architects, Grotta House 163
Robert A. M. Stern Architects, Roy E. Disney Animation
  Building 82
Robot Building, Bangkok 43
Rogers, Richard 177
Rossi, Aldo 83, 181
  Celebration Place 46
  Centro Direzionale e Commerciale Fontivegge 62
  Quartier Schützenstrasse 157
  Residence, Seaside 182
  San Cataldo Cemetery 181
  Scholastic Building 189
  Villa Alessi 54
Roy E. Disney Animation Building, Burbank 82

S
Safdie, Moshe, National Gallery of Canada 152
Saffarini, Adnan, Al Yaqoub Tower 136—7
St. Coletta School, Washington 120
St Mark's Road, London 146
Salon de Eventos, El Alto 32—3, 91
San Antonio Public Library 208
San Cataldo Cemetery, Modena 181
San Francisco Museum of Modern Art 93
Saville, Peter 76
Schijndel, Mart van, Oudhof 59
Scholastic Building, New York 189
The School of Slavonic and East European Studies,
  University College London 147
Schullin I jewelery store, Vienna 165
Scott Brown, Denise 52, 83
Short & Associates, The School of Slavonic and East
  European Studies 147
Silvestre, Freddy Mamani, Salon de Eventos 32—3, 91
SIS Building, London 124—5
SITE
  Best Products Showroom 130
  Best Store 90
Soeters van Eldonk Architecten, Piramides 16
Solpol Department Store, Wrocław 118
SOM, Chase Tower 73
Sottsass, Ettore
  The Acme House 128
  Casa Wolf 156
  David Kelley House 83
  Esprit Showroom 211
  Mourmans House 37
Spa School, London 186
Starck, Philippe, Groninger Museum 79
State of Illinois Center, Chicago 106—7
State University of Music and Performing Arts, Stuttgart 25
Steintor Bus and Tram Stop, Hanover 172
Stern, Robert A. M. 175
  Lang House 174
  Residence and Pool House 28
  Walt Disney World Casting Center 21
Stirling, James 25, 205
  Arthur M. Sackler Museum 115
Street Porter House, London 94
Studio Mutt, The Ordnance Pavilion 26
Suzan, Ayla, Kindergarten Wolfartsweier 70
Swan Hotel, Orlando 36
Syntax Building, Kyoto 74

T
Takamatsu, Shin
  Origin III 209
  Pharaoh Building 153
  Syntax Building 74
Tange, Kenzo, Tokyo Metropolitan Government Building 119
Taveira, Tomás, Amoreiras Apartments and Shopping Center
  184

Team Disney Building
   Orlando **14—15**
   Burbank **92**
Temasek Polytechnic, Singapore **99**
Terry Farrell & Partners
   Embankment Place **35**
   SIS Building **124—5**
   TV-am studios **58**
Thatcher, Margaret **8, 131**
Thematic House, London **114**
Thermes, Laura, Casa del Farmacista **20**
Thom Mayne, 2—4—6—8 House **129**
Tigerman, Stanley **134**
   The Anti-Cruelty Animal Shelter **134**
   Boardwalk **120**
   Urban Villa **78**
Ting 1, Örnsköldsvik **144—5**
Tokyo Metropolitan Government Building **119**
Toy Block House III, Tokyo **193**
Toy Block House IV, Tokyo **193**
Tozzo, Nino, Mosque and Islamic Cultural Center **52**
Tschumi, Bernard, Parc de la Villette **41**
Tusquets Blanca, Oscar
   Mas Abelló Housing Complex **154**
   Villa Andrea **133**
TV-am studios, London **58**
TVP Headquarters, Warsaw **148**
Twardowska, Maria, TVP Headquarters **148**

U
Umeda Sky Building, Osaka **65**
Ungerer, Tomi, Kindergarten Wolfartsweier **70**
Ungers, Oswald Mathias
   New Pumping Station Tiergarten **156**
   Villa Glashütte (Ungers House II) **63**
Union Bank of Switzerland, Basel **190**
United States Embassy, Lima **160—1**
Urban Villa, Berlin **78**

V
Vanna Venturi House, Philadelphia **112—13**
Venturi, Robert **7, 8, 9, 45, 49, 105, 141**
Venturi, Scott Brown and Associates
   Episcopal Academy Chapel **212**
   Franklin Court **89**
   Gordon Wu Hall **36**
   Museum of Contemporary Art **182**
   Provincial Capitol Building **167**
   Vanna Venturi House **112—13**
Villa Alessi, Verbania **54**
Villa Andrea, Barcelona **133**
Villa Glashütte (Ungers House II), Utscheid **63**
Village Hall, Windsor **102**

W
Wacoal Kojimachi Building, Tokyo **64**
Walala, Camille, Industry City Mural **27**
Wall House II, Groningen **128**
Walt Disney World Casting Center, Florida **21**
WAM Architecten, Hotel Zaandam **57**
Warhol, Andy **62, 93**
Warsaw University Library **88**
Watanabe, Makoto Sei, K-Museum **28**
Wilford, Michael, Arthur M. Sackler Museum **115**
Wilson, Tony **132**
Wines, James **31, 90**
   Best Products Showroom **130**
   Best Store **90**
Wingårdh Arkitektkontor, Ting 1 **144—5**
Winton Guest House, Owatonna **163**
Wolfe, Tom **41**
World Financial Center, New York **203**

Y
Yamasaki, Minoru, Helen L. DeRoy Auditorium **138**
Yamashita, Kazumasa, Face House **168**

Z
Zermani, Paolo, Casa Zermani **44**
Zevi, Bruno **167**

PICTURE CREDITS

Owen Hopkins

Owen Hopkins is Senior Curator at Sir John Soane's Museum, London where he leads the exhibitions and learning teams. Prior to that he was curator of the architecture program at the Royal Academy of Arts, London. His interests revolve around the interactions between architecture, politics, technology and society. He is curator of numerous exhibitions including most recently **Langlands & Bell: Degrees of Truth** (2020), **Eric Parry: Drawing** (2019), **Code Builder** (with Mamou-Mani Architects), **Out of Character** (with Studio MUTT), **The Return of the Past: Postmodernism in British Architecture** (all 2018) and **Adam Nathaniel Furman: The Roman Singularity** (2017). His previous books include **Lost Futures** (2017), **Mavericks** (2016) and **From the Shadows** (2015), **Architectural Styles** (2014) and **Reading Architecture** (2012). In addition to these authored works, he is editor of five volumes/series of essays and is a frequent commentator on architecture in the press, having written for a range of publications including **Dezeen**, **The Architectural Review**, **Domus**, **Blueprint** and **Icon**.

Author's acknowledgments

This book would have been inconceivable only a few years ago. Today, however, Postmodernism is no longer a dirty a word—or the style that must not be named—as a new generation of architects and designers have begun to reassess and reinterpret its ideals, tactics and aesthetics. One of the pioneers of this has been Adam Nathaniel Furman, whose tireless advocacy of color, ornament and aesthetic pluralism is a growing inspiration to many and has played a critical role in shaping this book. I would also like to thank Virginia McLeod at Phaidon for taking the leap to commission a book as bold and ambitious as this one, and Johanna and Dylan for putting up with me as it took shape.

Publisher's acknowledgments

The publisher would like to thank Jamie Ambrose, Vanessa Bird, Angelika Pirkl, Albino Tavares, and Rachel Ward, for their invaluable assistance in preparing this title.

Phaidon Press Limited
Regent's Wharf
All Saints Street
London N1 9PA

Phaidon Press Inc.
65 Bleecker Street
New York, NY 10012

phaidon.com

First published 2020
© 2020 Phaidon Press Limited

ISBN 978 0 7148 7812 6

A CIP catalog record for this book is available from the British Library and the Library of Congress.

Commissioning Editor: Virginia McLeod
Project Editor: Virginia McLeod
Production Controller: Jane Harman
Design: João Mota

Printed in China